ESCAPE
FROM
AMORGOS

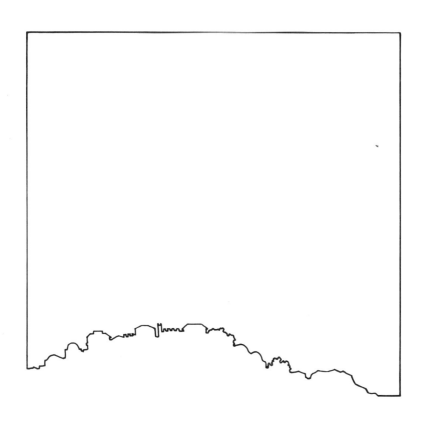

ESCAPE
FROM
AMORGOS

GEORGE MYLONAS

CHARLES SCRIBNER'S SONS · NEW YORK

Printed in the United States of America
Library of Congress Catalog Card Number 73-1352
ISBN 0-684-13729-1

CONTENTS

FOREWORD

This book dwells basically on the story of my arrest, imprisonment, exile, and escape from the clutches of the present Greek dictatorship. It also includes some information on contemporary Greek political history with which the average foreign reader is not familiar. And it tries to explain the dramatic plight of the Greek people, who have been subjugated to fascism in these latter years of post-war Europe after having valiantly fought against it in the forties, and having believed in the promises of their "great allies" about the "four freedoms" —promises that ended up with the deplorable association of the United States with the ruling military Junta.

Although a number of personal experiences are described in order to give the reader a sense of immediacy in approaching the Greek problem, this book is not an autobiography. I am in active politics and hope to be so for some years to come; I have not reached the time when I can look back and write my memoirs. In my fifty-third year, I look ahead. What I have written is a very rough sketch of my experiences, with politics as the center of gravity.

The life of any individual includes many personal and private experiences—happy, unhappy, or indifferent—that build up his own story, condition his feelings, define his reactions. They have been left out, except perhaps for some very slight indications. And so have most of the people, people who played and continue to play an important, sometimes a very important, role in my life. This book is about politics, and specifically, about a certain political adventure in my life— my escape.

Regarding my exile in Amorgos and the escape story, I am unfortunately obliged to avoid mentioning quite a number of fascinating facts and details, because I do not wish to endanger any of my fellow countrymen who still live in Greece under the dictatorship. Whatever I *do* write is true; I simply *don't write everything.* There are a few necessary and intentional alterations made in an attempt not to omit certain interesting episodes. Instead of completely sacrificing them, I have somewhat "troubled and dimmed the waters." Thus, there are cases where a man may appear as a woman, or vice-versa, a child take the form of an old man, a butcher be turned into a milkman, or confusion blur the description of places.

I would like to thank the wonderful people of Amorgos for their kindness and their perseverance. My fellow countrymen from Epirus, who in a hundred ways and through many dangers remembered me in Amorgos and now that I am abroad provide me with valuable connections within the country, I thank from the bottom of my heart. The day I live to return to Ioannina will be a great one in my life.

I express my gratitude to the small number of Greek and Italian friends—and especially to my daughter and her husband—whose invaluable aid made my escape possible.

I also take this opportunity to register my thanks to my distinguished Greek friends in Geneva who, with their kindness, their intelligence, and their humour, have made this second "exile" so much lighter for me to bear.

This book does not aspire to literary merits; nor is it a political treatise. It has been written directly in English as a narrative, not as a sociological analysis.

Finally, I would like to thank those few friends who were kind enough to read parts of my manuscript and offer valuable comments.

G. M.

Geneva, March 1973

ESCAPE
FROM
AMORGOS

1
ARREST

They came at 3:05 in the morning. I was sleeping lightly
and was aroused by the sound of footsteps on the gravel in the
garden of our house at Psychiko. I got up without putting on
the light and looked through the shutters; I saw a group of men
—there turned out to be fourteen—who had already jumped
the fence of our garden and were encircling the house. I put
on all the lights of the terrace outside, and they suddenly found
themselves illuminated, as if they had been expected. They rang
the bell insistently. I opened the door myself, in my pyjamas.
They were all in plain clothes, obviously members of the
régime's security police; probably one or two were in the
Army. I recognized only two plainclothesmen, who had been
following me about for the last two or three months. One of
them said, "Order of the government; you must follow us."
I was prepared, and I remarked ironically, "I suppose you have

an arrest warrant?" One of them, who turned out to be the local Psychiko security chief, forgot himself and said, "Well, Mr. Minister . . . you know," as if to say, "We are under an illegal régime; why bother asking for warrants?" By that time, my wife, Alex, and my son, Alexander, the only people in the house, had woken up and joined me. They were calm. I informed them, "These gentlemen will take me away." I was asked to dress. I went into my room. One of them came to the door and watched while I was dressing. They were quiet and stiff. They more or less invaded all the rooms, looking about, picking up a paper or just looking at a book, but I did not see them take anything with them.

I dressed and spoke briefly to my wife and son about the things they were to do after I left—routine, everyday matters. Following my captors out into the street, I saw four cars— one of them a black Morris, which had been trailing me about for days before my arrest. I was asked to get into one of the cars—as a matter of fact, that very Morris. There was a driver and a policeman next to him; in the back I sat between two policemen. All four cars (I never understood why there had to be such a procession) left in the darkness of the night. We were not going toward Athens but were heading toward the north, and I wondered where we were going. We didn't exchange a word.

At about 3:30 A.M. we reached a little square in the Athenian suburb of Nea Ionia, where the headquarters of the Security Police of the Athens suburbs are located. There was quite a martial atmosphere there: many jeeps, armed gendarmes, a few army trucks, all giving the impression that the square was actually occupied by an enemy force. We stopped before headquarters and I was told to get out. There was a group of about twenty gendarmes in uniform in front of the building. I walked through a line of them. They were silent. I was taken to a room, half-underground.

The door was opened and closed behind me.

I didn't have time to think much. Ten minutes later the door was unlocked and two gendarmes asked me to follow them. I was taken to a larger room with a table and three chairs and nothing else in it. It was summer, early in the morning of August 14, 1968. The window was open, but it had bars. I immediately noticed an armed guard in uniform outside the window. He just looked at me. I sat down and waited. A few minutes later the door opened and another arrested person, a general, came in.* Before the door had been closed, in walked two more military men under arrest.† I knew only one of them slightly, and we all addressed each other by our respective titles. We were already one chair short. We composed ourselves and started talking. At about 4:15 A.M. the door opened again, and in came Gerasimos Vassilatos, a member of Parliament for Athens of our party, the Centre Union, and a distinguished trial lawyer. He was about seventy and he told us that he was about to undergo an operation two days hence. Ten minutes later another man came in, the former director general of the Greek radio under the Centre Union Government, and a friend.‡ All these people had been arrested at their homes in the same manner as I.

It was about 5:00 in the morning and we were all beginning to be quite tired and sleepy, when in came another man.§ He walked with difficulty. He told us that he had been arrested the previous night at Xylokastro, where he was spending the summer with his family. He was suffering from a slipped disc and was in great pain. Time dragged on. No one came

* Major General George Koumanakos, a rightist but an able fighter and an opponent of the dictatorship.
† Wing Commander Deros of the Air Force and Captain Spyros Konofaos of the Navy.
‡ Sakis Peponis.
§ Brigadier-General Charilaos Tsepapadakis.

to tell us what we were accused of. At about 6:30 we were asked if we wanted to go to the toilet. We all went in turn down the corridor followed by two guards; the toilet door remained open. Afterwards we were given cups of coffee.

By now it was 8:00. One more arrested person arrived: Navy Commander Spyros Tapinis. Finally, at about 9:30 a gendarmerie lieutenant came in and told us, "You will be moved pretty soon," but he didn't say where. Ten minutes later an officer and three men in uniform arrived and asked three of us to follow them. We heard that they were being taken to the detention prison of Maroussi. At 11:00 three men and an officer took away the two naval officers and myself. When we came out into the square we saw a few onlookers, but the police were out in strength and the people were ordered to move along. We were told to enter a Landrover. The two naval officers stepped back and very politely and loudly said, "After you, Mr. Minister," a fact that obviously annoyed the security officers, who could not understand how any civilian, regardless of his rank, could come before the military, even though both were prisoners.

When we reached the Maroussi jail we were presented to a major of the Gendarmerie and, for the first time, were asked to give our names and identities. But still there was no accusation, and no answer to any of our questions. Three policemen took us to the first floor of the building, which was an old nineteenth-century country house transformed into a sort of prison with big iron bars installed in the windows. One large room contained twelve beds, another four, and, if I remember properly, there were two other rooms with three beds in each.

In one of the rooms there was a long table where we were to have our meals. The whole floor was closed off by one heavy door with bars, which had a small peephole through which a guard watched us constantly. A little while later, two more prisoners arrived from Nea Ionia. Also there were other friends who had been arrested by the Athens police and had been brought to the building a little before we had been.*

It was midday when the head guard came in. He told us a few things we should know. We could have no communication with our relatives. We would be permitted to go down into the yard for a walk twice a day. (Actually, we were only given permission once a day.) If there was something we wanted from our families, we could give him short notes to be read to them over the telephone. I remarked that I had no telephone at home because it had been cut off as a punishment from the first day of the dictatorship; it was therefore impossible for the police to reach my wife. I gave my mother's telephone number instead and sent a little note asking for some clothes, shaving equipment, and writing material. We had only the clothes we had pulled on in the middle of the night when we were arrested. I also asked for two books that I happened to be reading at the time: one, concerning the Greek revolution of 1821, was allowed me; the other was considered bad for me and I couldn't get it—Servan Schreiber's *Le Défi Américain* (*The American Challenge*).

Our first lunch was served by a woman who arrived with a big bowl of meat and potatoes. She was not permitted to come in unless accompanied by two gendarmes, obviously so we couldn't give her any messages. After lunch we sat on our beds talking away (I was in the twelve-bed room) about the political situation, about the events that had led up to the dictatorship, about the future.

That afternoon, as I was standing by the window, I saw my

* These were, as I recall: John Alevras and Philip Mavros, both members of Parliament for Athens in our party; Air Force General Andonakos; the journalist George Drosos; Captain of the Army Bouloukos; Naval Captain Costas Loundras; and Squadron Leader Goulas. Members of Parliament Xylouris and Koniotakis, and Admiral Rozakis were added to our lot that afternoon.

wife and son walking into the grounds. We had been forbidden to shout or make any sign to our relatives. However, I whistled a tune which my relatives recognised, and they immediately looked up. We saw each other for a second and I waved my hand. They had brought the things I had asked for, which they left with the officer in charge.

We were quite tired when we went to bed at nightfall. Our beds were very close. I was flanked by the Navy: Admiral Rozakis on my left and Captain Konofaos on my right. I slept soundly until 7:00 in the morning.

The next day was Thursday, August 15. It's a big holiday in Greece, the Feast of the Virgin Mary, and the name day of one of my daughters. There would be a feast at home, and there we were, separated from our families, for no legal reason and never told why. At about 9:30 we were permitted our first exercise in the little secluded area behind the building. The wall surrounding the court was over three metres high, so we couldn't see or be seen from outside. We couldn't escape the gendarmes with submachine guns who had been stationed in the four corners to intimidate us. I marched up and down at a quick pace. Because of the heart attack I had suffered a year earlier, a day without some exercise is bad for me. Perhaps I walked too quickly and abruptly because, I remember, I felt a slight itch in my back, which always means that I must be careful. I had my emergency pills with me and I was all right after a few minutes.

At 11:00 one of us, Captain Loundras, was called to report to the chief. He came back and said that he was being taken to the Athens security to see Lambrou. Lambrou was a somber figure, one of the chief torturers at the Athenian "Asphalia" (Security Police); we didn't like that news. Loundras never came back to Maroussi. We later learned that he was isolated and imprisoned in the big jail of Averoff, under the pretext that a gun had been found when they searched his house; it was an old pistol, a World War II souvenir. The real reason was, of course, that they wanted to blackmail his wife, Mrs. Eleni Vlachos, who was in London fighting the Junta. They didn't succeed; she never stopped fighting the dictatorship, although her husband remained in prison for thirteen months after that.

The first person to be called after Loundras was John Alevras. He quickly came back and told us he had been handed a piece of paper saying that he was being exiled to Aghios Efstratios, a very small island which had recently suffered from earthquakes, and where the living conditions were bad. He was told that he would be moved in a few days, but that they didn't know exactly when. Vassilatos was called next, to be told that he also was going to Aghios Efstratios; this was an especially harsh punishment for the old man, in view of his poor health. Then General Koumanakos was informed that he would be exiled to Parga, a small town in the northwest of Greece where conditions would not be bad. I was the fourth. I was handed a government order exiling me to the island of Amorgos in the Cyclades—a small, barren island I didn't know much about. This is what the order said:

Athens, 14 August, 1968. The Minister of Justice Ilias Kyriakopoulos and the Minister of Public Order Panayotis Tzevelekos, having in mind article 1 of the compulsory law of October 23, 1935, as amended by article 4 of law 167 of 1967, and having taken into consideration the facts against Mylonas which were given to us by the Security Services,* ordain that the said George Mylonas, son of Alexander, former member of Parliament, etc., who, through his actions in general, his contacts, and the way he expresses himself, is trying to bring about disorder in the security of the country and trying to induce other citizens to behave in the same way, be

* These "facts" were never specified; at least, I was never informed of them.

exiled to the island of Amorgos for six months. He will be granted the sum of 17 drachmas daily for his personal expenses [55 cents in American money]. No appeal is permitted against the present decision.

That was a dictatorship's justice: no specific accusation, no trial, no defense, not even a question asked, and a sentence simply issued at the will of the government. And no appeal was possible. I was told that I would be leaving Maroussi for Amorgos on August 19.

I returned to my comrades. No one knew very much about Amorgos. No one else was called to the office that day. Did that mean that only we four were to be exiled? The rest of the day was spent with a little reading, much talking and looking out of the window, and watching relatives come in with parcels. The guards repeatedly threatened to nail wooden planks on the windows if we made any sign of recognition to our families.

Vassilatos asked for a doctor. He said he would accept any doctor; it needn't be his own doctor necessarily but a military doctor or a doctor of the Gendarmerie. Another prisoner who had a broken leg made the same request. A little later that afternoon, one more arrested person was brought in. He was Squadron Commander Panayotis Diakoumatos, whom we will meet again much later in this book.

About 6:00 that evening I saw my son and wife arrive with a few additional things I had asked for. I and the other three people who had been given exile papers asked to see our families so that we could inform them of everyday matters that had to be taken care of at home and at our offices. We were not permitted to. Late that evening one more arrested man arrived, a member of Parliament for Piraeus of the Centre Union, John Papaspirou. He was immediately given an exile order for the small island of Tilos in the Dodecanese. That made five of us about to leave.

Quite late, at about 10:00 P.M., the door opened and a gendarmerie captain came in carrying a transistor radio. He said, "Look here, I can leave this with you if you want to hear the news; let's keep it between ourselves. I'll come and pick it up later." Then he left. We tuned in to the BBC and heard of our arrests and other news about Greece. That was the only way to find out what was happening in our country.

The next day, Friday, August 16, no doctor had appeared for the obviously sick Vassilatos. A few men left for places of exile. We had our usual morning stroll in the backyard. At about noon I saw my mother, an old lady of eighty-one, my wife and son, my eldest daughter, Maria, who was pregnant in her ninth month, and a friend whose name I had better not mention, standing outside in the street. I could see them, and happily they could see me, behind the bars. They must have understood that I was going to be moved somewhere far away, because I had requested that they bring me quite a number of items, including a lot of clothing; this proved to be a good indirect way of informing them. I wondered if they had been informed of my exile. I later found out they had not.

That afternoon one more arrested man was brought in. This time it was Stelios Allamanis, former minister and member of Parliament from Karditsa; he belonged to the so-called dissident group of the Centre Union, with which we were not on good terms. By that time there were twenty-one of us. The afternoon came: still no doctor. Vassilatos prepared a telegram which he addressed to the "Minister of Justice" and handed to the guards to be sent off; but nothing doing. In the evening, that captain brought his transistor again, and we heard the international news. (Did he do it because he wanted to be able to mention it one day if things changed, or did he do it because he was secretly anti-Junta?) My fellow detainees had a tendency to talk late into the night, and I was beginning to get quite tired. A little after midnight I felt the usual itch. I took a pill.

On the next day there were more announcements about where fellow detainees were to be exiled. Philip Mavros was to go to Kithyra; Xylouris and General Deros, to Katuna, a little village in the centre of Greece; Captain Konofaos was to go to Fourna, another forlorn village in the mountainous centre of Greece; Tapinis was being sent somewhere in Thessaly; Admiral Rozakis and Diakoumatos were to go to Karpenisi; Goulas, to Paksi. Six remained without deportation orders. Those of us who were about to leave insisted on seeing our families, but there was no answer to our repeated requests. Later, a negative answer was returned. That afternoon I was informed that I would be leaving on the ship *Despina* at 10:00 A.M. on Monday. But when I looked at the Athens daily newspaper that we had been handed, I could find no such voyage scheduled. I mentioned it to the officer later; he said he would look into the matter and let me know. The *Despina*, by the way, was a very old ship that went the rounds of the sparsely populated islands in the southern Aegean.

That afternoon I saw my son Alexander, again from afar. He brought something but was not permitted to contact me. I started wondering what he was doing about his trip to the United States. He had just finished high school and had been granted a scholarship and was preparing his papers for leaving. I hoped that my arrest would not create difficulties or that he would be denied a passport. Night came, and there was still no doctor for poor Vassilatos. Fortunately, his morale remained high.

The next day, August 18, more detainees left for their places of exile. From twenty-one, our number had been reduced to ten. At noon Lieutenant Spiliopoulos, one of our guards, told me that he had informed my family that I was leaving the next day and that they would be permitted to come to Piraeus harbour to say goodbye. A little later I was told that I was not leaving on the *Despina* but on the *Polikos,* at 3:00 P.M. I was forty-nine at the time, and both ships were probably older than I.

Next day was the day of my departure, my last day to see

Athens and Attica, where I had lived most of my life. I prepared my things, a valise and two parcels. Vassilatos was still without a doctor. He was to be taken the next day to Aghios Efstratios without having received medical care; happily, he outlived the affair. I had my last lunch with my friends. We toasted with water our quick liberation and the liberation of the country. At 1:30 it was time to leave. I was taken down to a brand-new, light blue car, a Morris once again, which belonged to the Gendarmerie; I noticed that it had a regular license plate in front and a gendarmerie plate in the back. Sloppy work! We crossed Athens. If anyone saw me who didn't know of my arrest, he would say, "Oh, there's George going down to the sea for a swim with three friends." The dictatorship was always careful about keeping up a façade.

At the port I learned that the *Polikos* was to depart later than scheduled. It had not yet arrived from a previous voyage and would not leave before 6:00. With the three men following me, I entered a café where my mother, my wife, my eldest daughter Maria, and my son Alexander sat waiting. The policemen remained at a table a little away from us, near the door. We sat together at the back of the café and discussed family matters. I heard that Alexander's trip to the States was coming up against difficulties. Soon my mother and daughter felt tired and emotionally overcome and were obliged to leave. Mother is very strong. She has seen much in her life: her father in politics, her husband in politics, and then myself, through all the tribulations of twentieth-century Greek history. She has stood up to it very well. The only thing she hopes is to live through it and see me back.

My wife and son stayed. Soon the time came. I pressed them to me. I boarded the ship. Flanked by two men, I stood on the deck to wave goodbye to my family. As the ship departed, we waved handkerchiefs, until finally I could see them no more. Who knew when we would meet again?

2
AMORGOS

The ship was almost empty. I read the newspapers for a while. At 8:00 we had our dinner in the ship's dining room. There wasn't anyone there who appeared to know me, and there we were, three people going on a trip! I was tired and went to my cabin about 9:30, after having stayed a bit on deck, looking at the sky. It was a very clear, starry night. I went to my berth and slept a little; when I woke up I saw that my two guards had not come into the cabin. They had settled themselves outside the cabin window on the deck. Were they being polite, wishing to spare me trouble, or were they making doubly sure that they didn't go to sleep? Anyway, there was no reason for them to be afraid of anything. Amorgos was to be the first port of call.

At 4:00 the next morning one of the two gendarmes who had been guarding me all night came in to say, "We have arrived." I was already awake. I got up, dressed, and went out on deck, but I couldn't see anything. It was a very dark night. Then, vaguely, I saw the shadow of a mountain; but there was not a single light. Finally, as the ship entered a small bay I saw one or two lights: the little port of Amorgos, called Katapola. A small boat drew alongside carrying two or three passengers who were leaving and three gendarmes in uniform. The gendarmes boarded the ship and started conversing with my two guards. They exchanged a few papers but never bothered to talk to me. Then we all got into the small boat, and a few minutes later I set foot on the soil of Amorgos. When would I leave it?

We entered a little café where I saw that there were electric light installations. I asked why the light wasn't on. I was told that it always went off at midnight. The ship blew its horn and left. The officer who had brought me and the officer who was taking charge of me exchanged papers—and then more papers. By this time dawn had come. From the window I saw a pretty little port and some white houses and assumed this was the place where I was to stay. But then I was told it was time to move. Outside there was a car, a Russian-made Volga station wagon. The five policemen, the civilian driver, and I got into the car and started up a rough dirt road. We rode for seven kilometres until we reached the top of the mountainous island, the little village of Hora, where I was to spend my period of exile. This village is the only one that has a road to the sea.

Like most Aegean islands, Amorgos is rather barren. It is very hilly and quite beautiful, but it is not as small as I had thought. It has eight villages in all, but they can only be reached by mule. I never saw them because I was not permitted to leave Hora, which is well built and quite picturesque. In the middle of the village there's a big rock with the remains of a castle. Some buildings, including churches, date back to the fourteenth or fifteenth century. Hora has about 120 houses, all whitewashed in the Cycladic manner, and quite a number of churches. There is, of course, no hotel. At that time, the village had electricity for sixteen hours a day.

The first place I was taken was the headquarters of the Gendarmerie of the village, in order to fill out a few forms. I entered the office and was introduced to the chief, a sergeant called Polychronopoulos (soon to be moved because of a nervous breakdown). Sergeant Polychronopoulos, who had six gendarmes under his command (my future guards), read out the conditions under which I would live. I was forbidden to go beyond the boundaries of the village. Within the village I was free. But, of course, I could not enter any of the houses of the villagers; I could only visit public places, such as the grocery store or the post office or the church. I would have to report to the police station every morning at 9:00 and every afternoon at 6:00 to sign in. I never understood why, since I was constantly followed, and my whereabouts were under the immediate supervision of the police. But I suppose that's part of dictatorial bureaucracy. I was told—a little vaguely—that relatives could come to see me from time to time. There were a number of things I could not do: I could not speak to any foreigner who might happen to be passing through the village. I could not speak to any state employees, which included civil servants and members of the Army, Navy, Air Force, and gendarmerie officers either in active service or retired. "Which means," I said, "that we won't speak to each other anymore." The sergeant didn't exactly get the joke. He said, "Well, you know, that doesn't mean me; it means people who come to the village." Reporters and press people were also completely out of bounds. It was then I heard that there was another exile in the village. He was an Army Brigadier-General named Rungieris, whom I did not know at all. But there were specific orders that we should never exchange a word. I tried to contradict the sergeant on this, saying that he was obviously misinterpreting some order; I knew of exiles on other islands who did speak to each other and even lived in the same house. He promised that he would ask his superiors for clarification. The clarification came two days later from his commander at Thira; it was, of course, to my detriment. I would not be permitted to address even a word to Brigadier Christos Rungieris. I met him a little later in the village and we nodded to each other. I liked his face.

Then the matter of finding a house for me came up. The village had roughly 250–300 inhabitants. I was not supposed to live in a house or use the room of a house inhabited by a local family. Therefore I had to rent a house that was empty. For just the first three days, I found a room on the basement floor of a house belonging to a woman who lived on the top floor with her son; there was no communication between the floors. A man was called in by the sergeant to see if I could rent a little second house he owned. I was stunned to see how frightened the man was when he was summoned by the police. When he heard that he was merely wanted to discuss renting his house, a look of relief came over his face that was really impressive.

The room I was in could not be used in winter; it had been an old shop in the basement of a building. Wind came in under the door and the toilet facilities were nonexistent. But I was soon to find out that this was the case with all the houses of Amorgos! After installing my valise and a few other things and resting a bit, I went out to see what the village looked like. Immediately I saw that I was under supervision. One of the policemen was strolling about near my house. He pretended that he didn't see me coming out, but I quickly realised that his presence there was no coincidence. Throughout my stay a guard was always around. Noontime came and I went for my lunch to a little tavern owned by a pleasant and friendly couple in their late fifties, Nikitas and Aspasia. The meals were very rudimentary. There was no question of any menu or choice. The meal was a sort of *plat du jour* which was ready and placed in front of you, and that's what you had to eat. I'm very flexible about eating and wasn't troubled at all. It was generally healthy food, usually products of the island. Sometimes there was a little fish. Meat—on the rare occasions it was served—was really bad. My first impression of the villagers was that they were kind and sympathetic: they obviously didn't like what was going on. They smiled very nicely when I met them in the little narrow streets.

I was lucky in finding a good house to live in. Four or five days after my arrival, I met a man, whom I vaguely remembered having seen in Athens, in the village square. He introduced himself and asked me how I happened to be here. When I explained, he expressed his sympathy. It turned out that he was a native of Amorgos, which he visited only occasionally. He owned a house on the island and offered me the key. I accepted his very generous offer, and a few days later established myself in his house, supposedly paying 350 drachmas monthly. My generous friend would not accept any rent, despite my insistence. The house was at least two hundred years old, with living quarters on the second floor. There were four rooms in all, which I did not need, and very little furniture. In the one room which I finally occupied was a bed, a few chairs, and a table. There was a little kitchen, but toilet facilities were nonexistent, aside from just a hole in the ground. There was no running water in the house, but there was an underground cistern that filled with rain water in the winter. Taking a bath was quite difficult. I used to pull up pails of water from the cistern in the basement and pour it all over me to wash. In the end, I got used to this system, and I even carried it on through the winter when it became bitterly cold.

3

FASCISM RETURNS
TO GREECE

Parliament had been dissolved on April 4, 1967, and a general election was called for May 28. The government then in power was a minority cabinet of the National Radical Union, or E.R.E. (the Greek conservative party), under Premier Panayotis Kanellopoulos. All indications showed that our Centre Union, under George Papandreou, was heading toward an electoral victory. The people were fanatically against a dissident group that had broken off from our party, called the "Apostates." I doubt whether they would have managed to elect a single deputy. The right-wing E. R. E. didn't seem to catch the imagination of any large segment of the voters. As for the E. D. A. (Left), it most likely would score something like its percentage in the previous election—around 12 percent of the vote.*

* My personal guess was that we would score something like 50 percent of the vote and get a comfortable majority in Parliament. But it

With elections set for May 28, people were getting somewhat excited; but there were no incidents. Everything was orderly. A big rally was being organized in Salonica in the north of Greece for Sunday, April 24. The leader of our party, George Papandreou, was planning to give his first pre-electoral speech there.

I had made plans to leave Athens on April 23 for Ioannina, my electoral area, where I would stay throughout the electoral period. The beautiful spring night of April 20 was as quiet as could be. At 4:30 A.M. or a little later, I was aroused by the telephone ringing at my bedside. It was a reporter from *Vima,* one of the Athenian papers that supported our party, giving me the news that the newspaper building had been surrounded by army units and tanks, and that obviously some sort of military coup was taking place. He then added, "Soldiers are coming right up the steps to my office now, and I'm hanging up." I tried to ring a few other people, but a few moments after that my phone didn't work. It had been cut as had all Athenian telephones to prevent any communication among the forces that could resist the coup. My wife happened to be away at the time, and my car was being repaired. The only other person in the house at the time was my seventeen-year-old son. I woke him and broke the news to him. It was already past

---

is interesting to note that most other forecasts were even more optimistic (from friends and foes alike). I was informed at the time that both the Greek and American Intelligence private popularity polls gave our party somewhere between 58–62 percent of the vote. The German magazine *Stern* predicted 55 percent. Savvas Konstandopoulos, the editor of the pro-régime paper par excellence, has since written, "the victory of the centre-left was a sure thing." And if the information of Elizabeth Drew in the *Atlantic* is correct, the U.S. State Department had allegedly rejected a proposal by the C.I.A. that the elections be rigged (through intimidation and falsification) because of doubts that such a plan would succeed in view of the great difference of votes between Centre and Right.

5:00 A.M. After trying in vain to communicate by telephone, we sat waiting. I had no doubts in my mind where the coup had come from. It was obviously from the Right, but I wasn't at all sure from which faction of the Right. I thought it probable that it had been perpetrated by the same group of reactionary Greeks surrounding the palace that had staged both the 1961 electoral fraud and the 1965 downfall of George Papandreou.

At about 6:00, I tried the radio: nothing but military music was being played. After a little while, a voice announced that martial law had been proclaimed all over the country, all articles of the Constitution relating to human rights, political freedom, elections, etc., had been suspended, and that a decree to that effect had been signed by the King and the government. It didn't say which government, and one was led to believe that it was the Kanellopoulos Government that had declared martial law. I didn't consider that very probable; it looked like a military coup by the rightist officers. It was later proved that the decree was signed by a group of army colonels who called themselves the "government," and that it had never been countersigned by the King. The declaration of martial law was a purely dictatorial act carried out by a military junta, and aimed primarily at stopping the elections from taking place.

At about 7:00 we went out. Everything seemed rather calm in the suburb of Psychiko, where we lived. We talked to neighbors. No one seemed to know more than the fact that tanks had occupied the centre of Athens and that a dictatorship had been declared. Sometime afterwards, as I was in my garden talking over the wall with neighbours, I saw the King's car pass. He was driving, but there were five army officers with him, two in front and three at the back. I didn't recognise any of them. The King seemed to be driving toward the home of his mother Queen Frederika, which was about a kilometre away. The picture was odd: it gave the impression that the man had practically been abducted. He didn't see me; he looked very pale, and he had a frown on his face.

A little later I walked to Andreas Papandreou's house, about a kilometre's walk. I saw the glass pane of the entrance broken. I went up the steps feeling uneasy and rang the bell. His American-born wife, Margaret, opened the door. She was obviously very upset and told me what had happened during the night. A group of military men had charged into their house at about 2:30 A.M. and had taken Andreas away by force, after he had been wounded jumping from a terrace on which he had taken refuge. He was obliged to come out from hiding when the military threatened to shoot his son George under his very eyes! Margaret didn't know where her husband was. She told me that her father-in-law, George Papandreou, had also been taken away from his house at Kastri. Andreas's old mother, Madame Sophia, whom I had known since I was a boy, was quite composed but obviously very anxious. Besides the four children, Margaret's father and mother from America and another American lady friend were staying with them. They had all witnessed the scene: the threat on the boy's life, Andreas's arrest, the brutality of the military. We talked matters over and promised to keep in contact. At about noon I returned home.

By that time, news was coming in indicating that a group of army colonels, people completely unknown, had seized power by force. The Papandreous, a number of politicians from our party, Prime Minister Kanellopoulos, and some of his principal ministers had been arrested. A great many other arrests had taken place during the night, especially among the rank and file of the Left and the Centre, in Athens and in other parts of Greece. The King's attitude was uncertain. At about 5:30 in the afternoon we heard over the radio that a new government had been formed, presided over by the Public Prosecutor to the Supreme Court, Constantine Kollias. A very bad omen! Kollias was a judge with a bad reputation. He was an extreme rightist, the man who had intervened to try to cover up the defendants in the Lambrakis murder trial in Salonika. He was a man whom we progressives considered to have no scruples or dignity. The other members of the government were only three: a certain Colonel George Papadopoulos, who became Minister to the Premier, one Brigadier Stylianos Pattakos, who became Minister of the Interior, and another unknown colonel, Nicholas Makarezos, who became Minister of Economic Coordination. The other posts remained vacant.

After having exchanged all sorts of information and rumours with a few friends, neighbours, etc., and having in vain tried to communicate by messenger with certain people, I went to see Mrs. Papandreou again. I think it was then that she told me that she had had news that Andreas was in good health and was being detained in a small hotel in Pikermi, some twenty miles from Athens, with other politicians. During the day, one or two friends of Andreas had visited her, but the greak bulk of our followers had more or less vanished. That was quite a surprise to us, and it explained how little prepared the big mass of Centre Union voters was for any sort of dynamic confrontation. They believed in democracy and in victory through the ballot-box.

As the night was setting in, I felt that it was my duty to stay at the Papandreou home; I didn't think I should leave the women and children alone. Margaret accepted my proposal. I went home, got my son, and returned to the Papandreous sometime after the curfew time had started. We had dinner there and talked matters over. We wondered what might happen that night; a search of the house, for instance, for "incriminating" documents. But we couldn't do anything about it at that time. We all went to bed exhausted. My son and I slept in Andreas's office on the third floor. The night went by without incident.

Next day, we returned home. More news was coming in. A very small group of army officers in key positions had managed to seize control of the armed forces and take everyone by surprise. They had simply applied an existing emergency plan code-named "Prometheus," which had been prepared by the NATO General Staff to be used in case of war. The plan had been adapted by the insurgents to round up all sorts of people, from right to left, who would be the natural opponents of a dictatorship. Many of the army units in the provinces applied "Prometheus" when they got the order from Athens (after the defection to the Junta of General Spandidakis, who was Chief of the Army General Staff), without even knowing what it was all about. Thus, the Junta managed to seize power with practically no bloodshed. There were about eight or ten people killed in the process, including a young girl (who, not knowing what had happened, was fired at by a tank in the early hours of April 21 in Athens as she emerged on the street to catch a train), an army officer and a sergeant who resisted the insurgents, a detainee at the Athens race track prisoners' assembly point, and a few others.

How can one explain this easy, virtually unopposed putsch, by a group of not more than forty or forty-five army officers from a total of 10,000?

After the fall of the Stephanopoulos Government (late December 1966) and the formation of the Paraskevopoulos caretaker cabinet that was to hold the elections of May 28, 1967, the so-called Big Junta was secretly created. It was composed of the "cream" of Greek reaction: certain generals, extreme rightist elements in E. R. E., certain members of the economic oligarchy, and a few other personalities in close contact with Queen-Mother Frederika. This Big Junta was preparing a legal-looking coup, so to speak, based on an article of the Greek Constitution which states that in case of "obvious foreign or internal threat" to the security of the country, the temporary suspension of a number of articles of the Constitution related to human rights, free speech, elections, etc., can be ordained by the government. This decree has to be ratified by Parliament within fifteen days. (In the outgoing Parliament, E. R. E. and the Apostates put together had a slight majority.)

King Constantine had certain doubts as to the advisability of this undertaking, and thus the date of this coup was postponed two or three times. The dynamic forces that were to be used for the coup were the "colonels" who held the key positions in the Army General Staff and the K. Y. P. (Greek C.I.A.) and some of the commanders of the crack troops in the Attica plain surrounding Athens. One cannot, for the time being, pin down the exact procedure of the transfer of the principal responsibility for the coup from the Big Junta to the Colonels. It can be convincingly argued that the U. S. secret services controlling the Colonels, worried by the King's and the generals' hesitancy, considered that they were the best group to apply the Prometheus Plan. It is also logical to believe that the Colonels themselves, nourishing feelings of frustration and enmity toward the generals, took advantage of the indecisiveness of the Big Junta to grab power and use it for their own ends. A number of books and a few hundred articles have been written on the subject, supporting several different viewpoints.* Surely when the day of liberation comes, many inter-

* The recent revelations of P. Papaligouras (the Minister of Defense in the Kanellopoulos Government), N. Makarezos, and Gregory Spandidakis seem to support my point of view along the following lines: a) The pre-Junta reactionary establishment was planning to use the device of article 91 of the Constitution (Papaligouras); b) the Prometheus Plan was applied earlier than planned due to the "haste of the Colonels" (Spandidakis). What does not emerge from the statements of these men, but is historically factual, is that General Zoitakis—who was later named Regent by the military régime—defected. He was a member of the Big Junta and he informed Colonel Papadopoulos of all its plans, movements, decisions, and doubts. General Spandidakis finally sided with the Colonels and issued orders to the army units to move and apply the Prometheus Plan.

esting and important facts concerning the dramatic events that led up to the April 21 coup will come to light.

No newspapers were published on the morning or the afternoon of the twenty-first, but on April 22 the first censored press appeared. A number of papers stopped publication altogether. The censored press uniformly gave the Junta's point of view: the nation was saved from Communism and from the danger of disorders. But even on that first day there was already the promise—which was never made good and never will be— that democratic order would be re-established as soon as possible. Needless to say, the allegations of the Junta about the existence of a Communist danger of any sort, let alone the threat of a takeover, have been denied by all the responsible people of the day, including the King, and since then, by the dictator Papadopoulos himself more than once. "The danger to Greece does not lie in Communism," Papadopoulos has said, "but in the anarchism of the western European democracies." The only "threat" that really existed, and which the Junta wanted by all means to avert, was the threat of the electoral victory of the Centre Union, which might have fully re-established the democratic régime of the country and eliminated the water-tight compartments within which the Right could operate, such as the armed forces and foreign policy departments, and the remnants of the parastate forces of the Right that had not been fully abolished during the "spring" of 1964–65.

Two days later, a picture showing the heads of the new government appeared in the press. A few more ministers had been named; all were unknown. None belonged to the existing political parties. The Minister of Public Order, a certain Paul Totomis, did not have a clear record and was a known agent of the C. I. A. (Recently, Jack Anderson, the American columnist, actually accused him of embezzlement.) The King stood moodily in the middle. Unhappily, he had given in to the Colonels (and to his mother?) and had finally sworn in the new government, although it remained a fact that he had not signed the revolutionary decree of April 21. From that moment on, and until his abortive attempt to overthrow the Colonels in December 1967, in the minds of most people he was identified with the dictatorship.

It was clear that the Americans in Greece were far from being unhappy with this affair. All that can be said for them is that perhaps there were a few who were opposed; but by and large the American serviceman or embassy employee or C. I. A. agent didn't make any bones about showing his pleasure that the elections and a Centre Union victory had been averted. I think it was the third or fourth day of the dictatorship that I visited a lady first secretary of the U. S. Embassy at her home in Psychiko, and I was really taken aback by the cynical attitude with which events were being interpreted—along the "let's give the Colonels a chance" line. I suppose that with visitors who did not express their antidictatorial views as clearly as I did, the American attitude was even cruder.

I have heard that most of the political officers of the American Embassy in Athens at the time denied that the embassy as such had any knowledge of the April 21 military coup. Ambassador Talbot assured me of this personally in March 1970 in New York. However, American diplomats generally accept the fact that the United States at first "put up" with the coup and gradually reverted to full support of the Junta, with increased miliary aid, loans, support in international organizations, etc.; this constituted a decisive factor in the continuation of the military dictatorship in Greece. And they accept the view that a withdrawal of American support would bring about the fall of the régime.*

* See Nicholas Gage and Elias Kulukundis in *The American Scholar*, vol. 39, no. 3, summer 1970, p. 480. An American diplomat in Athens

The U.S. administration mistrusted most Greeks who did not belong to the Right. The American military establishment and the C.I.A. had very close links with the Greek Army, which, ever since the civil war of 1947–49, they had considered as "their baby." A number of known American agents (Papadopoulos, Totomis, Androutsopoulos, Angelis, Tom Pappas, Farmakis, and others) acquired great power as soon as the Junta overthrew the parliamentary régime. American military and C.I.A. personnel in Greece (to mention only two: NATO Admiral Rivero and Potts, a C.I.A. man) openly expressed their pleasure at the coup. If one also bears in mind C.I.A. military interventions in Guatemala and Cuba, a strange meeting in Washington of high U.S. officials in February 1967 in which a decision was taken not to forestall the coup,* the

---

says: "If Washington decided that this regime is bad for Greece, bad for the NATO alliance, bad for this section of the world, and said so publicly, I think the Junta would topple."

* See the *Washington Post*, May 15, 1967: "As it turned out, the top-secret meeting in Washington in mid-February was like the lament of a Greek chorus for the tragedy to come. Around the table were military, intelligence, state—all the powers dealing with the Greek problem. C.I.A. reports had left no doubt that a military coup was in the making with the knowledge if not the sanction of King Constantine. It could hardly have been a secret. Since 1947 the Greek army and American military aid group in Athens, numbering several hundred, have worked as part of the same team. The team has spent something under $2 billion on the guns, planes, tanks and ships of the Greek forces.

"The solemn question was whether by some subtle political intervention the coup could not be prevented. Could parliamentary government be saved? . . .

"The consensus around the table, after some handwringing with agonized appraisals of the consequences, was that no course of action was feasible. As one of the senior civilians present recalls it, Walt Rostow, the President's advisor on national security affairs, closed the meeting with these words: 'I hope you understand, gentlemen, that what we have concluded here, or rather have failed to conclude, makes the future course of events in Greece inevitable.' "

pressure exercised on America's European allies in favor of the Junta, and the warm friendship of Vice-President Agnew towards the dictatorship, to mention only a few of the odd "coincidences," it is clear that the United States probably organised, certainly accepted, and has since openly supported the April 21 putsch and the military dictatorship which ensued.

On the fifth day of the dictatorship, my telephone service was restored; but it didn't last long. On May 5, it was cut off again, never to be reconnected. I remained without a telephone during all the months preceding my final arrest. At the beginning I was followed, but not every day and not regularly. There was usually a man outside the door strolling up and down, and sometimes a car followed me. During these first months, however, it wasn't very difficult to get out of range, so to speak, by means of a few rather classic tricks: entering a house that had two exits, changing taxis, etc. Practically everyone was shocked and unhappy with the situation, and the government didn't manage to acquire any popularity. During the first weeks of the dictatorship, the events that unfolded were like scenes in a tragicomedy.

But then disturbing and often tragic stories started coming in, one after the other. People were arrested in their beds. People were arrested in parks. People were arrested in their offices. In the central hall of the National Bank, one man was arrested by the Security Police while his colleagues and clients watched his abduction dumbfounded. If anyone was a bit late getting home, his family suffered agonies.

Some of those arrested returned home within four or five days. They had a haggard look in their eyes, and more often than not the clear signs of torture on their bodies. I heard of two cases of men who turned up naked at their homes in the working class suburbs around Athens. Before sending them home, their torturers, who had taken their clothes, had bound their eyes and pretended that an execution was about to take place. Of the five security services (the Military Police, the Security Police, the regular City Police, the K.Y.P. (C.I.A.), and the Gendarmerie), the Gendarmerie was the least ferocious, and there were a number of cases of humane treatment within its ranks, and even expressions of hatred of the dictatorship. Members of the Gendarmerie helped people get home and advised them, in their own interests, to keep their mouths shut about their "unique" adventures.

Mr. M. was the owner of a small shop who loved to spend his free time in politics. He was the type of person who becomes a member of all sorts of clubs and committees, who loves to prepare resolutions, and who is happy when he can deliver an address. His political leanings were vaguely centre-leftist. One evening as he was returning home, he was recognised by two plainclothesmen who, before the dictatorship, used to attend all labour, student, or political gatherings. He was taken to the Security, where he was locked up in a small cell without a window and without light. For forty-eight hours he wasn't allowed outside, nor did anyone answer his shouts and pounding on the cell door. After some time, he was obliged to defecate on the floor, and he remained in that stench, without any food or water, for two days. Fortunately, his was what one might call a mild case; he was released. When he got home he left immediately for a clinic in order to recuperate, but also so that he could get as far away as possible from the thugs of the Junta.

The wives of the Junta's prisoners were in a sense worse off than those who, by the thousands, were being sent to a concentration camp on the uninhabited island of Yiaros. In a way these prisoners were the freest citizens of Greece! They openly and loudly discussed politics, they insulted the dictatorship, and once, when one official, Vice-Premier Pattakos, had the cheek to go and review the camp, they shouted to him, "Who are you, and who gave you the right to pose as the Greek Government?" But the women lived with uncertainty: the future was unknown; salaries had suddenly stopped; offices were closed down; debts were mounting.

An acquaintance of mine, the mayor of a small town, was arrested and shipped to Yiaros. His wife, in despair, went to see the government's local administrative representative, or Nomarch. She asked him if he was aware that her husband had been a conscientious mayor, impartial in carrying out his duties, and that he had been elected by a large majority. The Nomarch put up his hands: "Madam, I can do nothing. It was your husband's fault. Why did he have to enter politics? Politics is not a good thing for family men!" What the Nomarch did not say was that the mayor was arrested *because* he had been elected by a large majority. Any elected authority was anathema to the Colonels.

But in all this tragedy that suddenly befell the Greek people, comedy had its share.

A university professor, known for his democratic ideals, but in no way politically active and in rather poor health, lived in constant fear of arrest. He stayed away from his house all day so that he would not be found if the Security Police came. At night, not wishing to stay in another house and incriminate friends (it was a serious crime punishable by imprisonment for up to eight years if you gave hospitality to anyone in your home without first getting special permission from the police), the professor returned home. One evening when he got home the doorman of his apartment house told him that an army officer had asked for him during the day. The professor spent an agitated and sleepless night. The next day he went to the university, where a group of students were waiting for him to take their final oral exam. Among them was a young reservist second lieutenant. The officer approached the professor and very politely asked him if he could take the exam right away, because he had been appointed to a unit far from the university and was obliged to leave at noon. "I came to ask you for this favour yesterday," said the second lieutenant, "but you were not home." With a sigh of relief, the professor answered, "I will do it gladly, but my dear man, what a time you chose to visit people's homes in uniform!"

Other friends in the academic community told me that more than once, while correcting exam papers, they would come across phrases like this: "I am a good soldier in an armoured unit and I helped save the fatherland on April 21. Please therefore overlook the mistakes in this paper." The worst of it is that many professors gave in to such subtle blackmail for fear of arrest.

One heartening factor during those first weeks of the dictatorship was that the military were far from being all with the Junta. A friend of mine who came from Corinth to Athens the day after the coup told me that at a certain point on the way the bus was stopped and the passengers' identities were checked by a group of student reservist officers of the Artillery School. The students were benumbed and pitiful, and avoided looking the passengers in the eyes. They knew that what they had been instructed to do was illegal.

Other friends, who were arrested on the first day of the coup, told me that the army officers who were holding them in a camp at Piraeus didn't hide their dissatisfaction with what was going on. "Don't worry," they said, "this is pure insanity; it cannot last more than a week."

But it has lasted six years! This shows the importance of holding the levers of control in a modern community. The power of the modern state has acquired huge dimensions, and the means at its disposal are capable of eliminating all forms of privacy. And if state leadership falls into the wrong hands by force, its destructive power becomes immense. And yet the Greek dictatorship does not feel secure: more than 3,500 armed forces officers have been fired since the coup!

For many days no foreign papers were permitted to circulate in Greece. When indignation abroad gradually subsided, foreign papers appeared again, but pages referring to Greece were torn out. After a few weeks, when the Junta saw that anti-dictatorial news in the foreign press could not in itself create a popular revolt, foreign papers could be bought in the central newsstands in Athens. This helped the régime's façade: and after all, how many Greeks dared buy or could read foreign newspapers?

As for the Greek papers which continued publication, their chief characteristic was boring uniformity. They were not only censored, they were told what to write and in what form, and where to position it on a given page. The praise of the wonderful Colonels' régime reached a crescendo.

The Greeks are an extroverted people, and they use their voices a lot and loudly; now they were morose and spoke in whispers. Summer had settled in, and in the evenings, in the open-air cafés, no one could hear what was being said at the next table. Discussions took place, but very quietly. Everyone was saying the same thing, but each group was afraid of its neighbours.

People could be seen being abducted and dumped into police cars, and the passersby would hardly dare give more than a quick glance. At night one could hear the insistent ringing of a bell and kicks at the closed door of an apartment; no other tenants would look out to see what it was all about. They knew. And if an optimist telephoned the police to say that a group of unknown individuals, not in uniform, were trying to break into an apartment, he would get the sibylline answer: "Don't worry, it's nothing serious."

The people were frozen. But they were not unwilling to help. I did not hear of a single case, among the thousands of people who were arrested or fired from their jobs, of someone running into trouble with his landlord because he could not pay rent. On the contrary, a hidden wave of compassion and solidarity rose in the enslaved land. One person took care of the children of an exile; another hid his precious books before they were seized by the police; a third would hide a persecuted person, despite the great danger in which he placed himself, feeling pride and deep satisfaction when he heard over the radio the threats against those who gave asylum to enemies of the régime.

And the arrests continued. Some ended in torture, long imprisonment, and, occasionally, mock trials. Others were purely for purposes of intimidation. There was a great variety of arrest techniques. The simplest form was a written invitation, usually delivered at dawn, for someone to appear before the police "on a matter concerning you," at 3:00 P.M., for instance. By the time the arrested man reported, he would already be extremely nervous and ready for the worst. He could be made to wait (usually alone in an empty room) for as long as two or three hours. Then the arrested man might be called in before an icy officer who would slowly and meticulously take down his identity items (which he obviously knew very well anyway), down to the birthdate of his grandmother). Then he would be sent back to the waiting room for another hour or two. All sorts of noises, harsh orders, cries, etc., would in the meantime contribute to his demoralization. About 10:00 P.M. he might be taken in to another officer, who would politely offer him a cup of coffee and "advise" him in a friendly way to watch his step because they had information he was not very faithful to the national government. He might try to answer, explain, ask a question, but the officer would take no heed. He would then suddenly rise and tell the man that he was free to go home, but that next time it would not be so easy. He would ring a bell and nod to a policeman who, instead of taking him to the outer door, would lock him up in a cell. If he protested, the policeman would calmly answer that those were his orders. And then, after a terrible sleepless night, the man would be freed next morning, without any futher explanation. He had not been detained twenty-four hours, nor had he been mistreated, but what an experience! Anyone would have to be a hero to indulge in anti-government activities after that. And yet so many did.

In the meantime the arrested man's family would be in a state of terrible anxiety. When he had not returned by 8:00 or 9:00 P.M., his wife would most likely have called the police office to which he had been ordered to report. She would be told that no such person was there. She would insist, saying her husband had received a written order to appear there. The officer would answer that he was sorry, there was obviously some mistake; no such person was being held or had been asked to report to the police station. The Kafkaesque tragedy would mount when the wife would later contact the central headquarters of the police, to be reassured that the matter would be looked into and she would be called back. The phone would ring at 1:00 A.M., and she would dash to it full of anxiety, only to be told by a suave voice that Mr. So-and-So, about whom she had inquired, was a bank employee who lived at No. 5 such-and-such a street, where he could be found (the very address where she was calling from!). She would try hopelessly to respond, but the connection would be cut off.

But there was much worse than that: days in prison without any explanation; beatings, threats, and tortures, including electric shock, deprivation of food and water, whipping the soles of the feet, kicking in the testicles and face, and so on. There were a number of actual murders. I know of twelve certain cases, but the figure is probably nearer twenty.*

* See Appendix A, p. 197 for excerpts from available accounts of the Junta's numerous tortures. As has been officially proved through the Report of the European Commission on Human Rights to the Council of Europe (a 1,200-page document published in 1969), the Junta Government practised torture in its prisons as a matter of course. The

And yet in the midst of this tragic atmosphere oddly enough another disease spread: optimism. No one believed the dictatorship could possibly survive; it was much too unpopular. During the first two years at least, the average Greek believed in the "certain fall of the Junta within the next three to six months." And this contagious optimism spread from lip to ear throughout the country and, I believe, in the last analysis played an important role in bringing about the lack of a well-organized resistance. But optimism is part of the Greek character.

It was in the last days of May 1967 that a few men, including myself, met and founded the resistance organisation that has since come to be well known: Democratic Defense. It was composed of men and women coming from what was called the Centre-Left in Greece: certain individuals belonging to five more or less distinct groups, and that's why its governing board is always composed of five members, although the organisation has long since grown into a unified body; and no one really remembers from which of these groups, or outside of these, its members come from. They were: the "Papanastasiou Club," named after a distinguished Greek Social-Democrat of the 1920's; the so-called Democratic Clubs in which people of the professions and of the arts participated with a view to helping political progress in Greece; the small Greek Socialist-Democratic Union, an organization militating for the creation of a Socialist Party; a group of university students connected with the Centre Union's youth movement; and, finally, a restricted number of Centre Union members of Parliament of progressive centre-leftist orientation. The first leadership or directing board of Democratic Defence was elected in the underground of a

---

Council of Europe (a body comprising the eighteen democratic nations of Western Europe), after carefully weighing the evidence for over a year and making doubly sure that the régime had violated all human rights, finally, on December 13, 1969, decided to expel Greece from its ranks.

little house on Mt. Lycabettus. Unhappily, it is not advisable at this time to give their names. I was one of them, and ever since that first meeting, I have been recognized as the political representative of the organisation.

Our plan was simple—resistance against the dictatorship by all possible means. We would meet about once a week, taking great precautions. We met at the unlikeliest places in Athens and its suburbs and, fortunately, we were never found out. We got things running quite well. We quickly established an illegal press and issued a bulletin that appeared rather irregularly, calling for resistance.*

Arrests soon began taking place. The first serious arrest was that of Gerasimos Notaras and his group, in the fall of 1967. Later, a group of our members in Salonika—Paul Zannas, Stelios Nestor, and others—were arrested. More arrests had taken place in Athens by the summer of 1968, and that was the time that Vassilis Filias, Spyros Plaskovitis, and myself were arrested, too. There have been four major trials of members of the Democratic Defence (two in 1968, one in 1969, and one in 1970); since the Junta, despite the tortures, did not manage to get to the bottom of everything, I will not mention here the names of all our arrested comrades. I can only cite the figure of 137 men and women seized from 1967 to early 1972. Resistance can't be carried out without victims!

I was never personally brought to trial or mistreated. The Junta usually avoided bringing former members of Parliament to a court-martial for fear of adverse publicity. For example, they knew Mikis Theodorakis was the leader of the Patriotic Front; they did not try him, although he was in their hands for two years. They knew of Andreas Papandreou's pre-eminent role in resistance, but he was kept in prison and never tried. They knew very well of my involvement in Democratic Defence, but they chose to send me to exile, not to

* See Appendix B, p. 212, for full text of the first proclamation.

try me. There were some exceptions, however. The most notable took place at a time the Colonels wanted to appear strong after their ouster from the Council of Europe: the trial and sentencing to four and a half years of imprisonment of the distinguished member of Parliament and former Centre Union minister, John Zigdis.

Two other resistance organisations were formed more or less at the same time. One, belonging to the Centre and called D.E.K.A., was quickly decimated; its members were arrested, and the organisation ceased to exist. The other organisation, which has consistently been going strong, was called P.A.M. (the Patriotic Front) and belonged to the Left. Mikis Theodorakis was one of its principal figures. A conversation between the representatives of our two organisations was arranged to take place in August 1967. Mikis Theodorakis, who was in hiding, would be the representative of P.A.M.; and I, usually followed about by plainclothesmen, would represent Democratic Defence. The meeting had been arranged, if I remember correctly, for August 21 or 22, 1967. On August 17 I suffered a mildly serious heart attack that obliged me to stay in bed for quite a while. George Loulis, the late member of Parliament for Volos and a dear friend, substituted for me. He and Mikis Theodorakis met. A very few days after that, both men, together with a number of other P.A.M. people, were arrested.

After these arrests we made contact again; it wasn't easy. In November 1967 two secret meetings between myself and two representatives of P.A.M., Katy Zevgou and Tassos Demou (both then in hiding), took place, in the very heart of Athens, after great precautions.* We switched means of trans-

---

* Mrs. Zevgou, whose leftist husband had been assassinated in Salonica in the middle forties, managed to escape from Greece without ever having been recognized (1971). So did Demou, a journalist, more recently (1972).

portation, entered houses, went out of houses, and finally met at a place where no one could possibly find us. We had long conversations and finally signed the first agreement of co-operation between resistance organisations.* This coopera-tion has been going on ever since in a friendly and brotherly spirit.

That brings us to December 1967, when the King, who by then had obviously understood his grave error in recognising the Colonels, staged his counter-coup. It was a badly prepared operation, having been betrayed at many levels, and it was easy for the Colonels to get the better of their opponents. In the early hours of December 14, the day after his abortive coup, the King was obliged to flee the country from Kavala, in the north of Greece, and take refuge in Rome, where he has remained ever since. Although the King was far from liked for a number of reasons, his coup became popular in the north of Greece where he actually staged it. The city of Kavala, for instance, which is a leftist stronghold, gave him an ovation when he appeared on a balcony denouncing the Junta and the military government. It was a dream that lasted only a few hours.

It should be made clear that the King did not automatically capture the people's heart through his anti-coup. The roots of popular mistrust of his person—and of the crown—are very deep. But the Greek people, with their intelligence and keen political sensitivity, know clearly who their basic enemy is, and they exploit any occasion offered to hint at, or express their aversion for, the military dictatorship. In the case of Kavala, the popular manifestations did not mean a sudden love for Constantine, but symbolised the people's absolute en-

* The text of the communiqué, which was published in the under-ground press in February 1968, is reproduced in full in Appendix C, p. 217.

mity for the Junta, and indicated tolerance toward someone who, at a given moment, showed opposition to the Colonels' régime. This spirit of guarded toleration toward the King seems to have finalised his decision to refuse any cooperation with the Junta. This attitude could possibly be changed to sympathy if Constantine abandoned his somewhat neutral position and publicly expressed his opposition to the dictatorship.

In Athens, the counter-coup didn't disrupt ordinary life, which went on more or less as usual under the Junta. At about 5:00 P.M. of the day it took place I decided it would be better if I vanished. There was a rather good possibility that there would be many arrests on this occasion.

As a first step, I left my house and went out to Kiphisia, where my mother, daughter, and brother lived. But I didn't stay there long; a few minutes after I arrived I got a message from my son Alexander. We had no telephone at home, but he had managed very intelligently to get out of the house to warn me: "They have come for you here at Psychiko." About 5:30 a detachment of police and army men went to my house in order to arrest me. My wife told them that I wasn't there. They searched the house and didn't find me.

After that I thought it would be best to leave my mother's house too. Having made previous arrangements with two friends in case of danger, I left in someone else's car and went to Athens. I took refuge in the house of one friend for two days and then shifted to another friend's house, which was safer. It is interesting to note that as I was leaving my mother's house—I don't suppose that I was more than two hundred yards away—the police turned up and searched it thoroughly. They had missed me by not more than a minute or two.

The King's coup utterly failed. Many arrests took place that night, including a great number of former members of Parliament. I remained in hiding. Remaining in hiding in a house for some time can become pretty hard. The place belonged to a couple with no children and no housemaid, and that made matters simpler. They both left the house during the day to work. I would stay in the house, as a matter of fact in one room. I never went near the window because the house was in the centre of Athens and I might be seen. I never answered the phone or the doorbell if it rang while they were away. When they returned in the evening things were more pleasant; we would talk and have dinner together; but whenever the doorbell rang, I was quickly locked up in my room. It wasn't anything terrible but it wasn't a happy period in any way, and it could have become very gruelling if I had remained there for long. I did manage to communicate with my home through an intermediary who was not under suspicion.

While I was in hiding, I had to contact my friends in Democratic Defense to see what steps we should take to coordinate our actions. Using the phone was, of course, out of the question. So I sent messages to Vassilis Filias through three consecutive couriers, and it was agreed that I would meet him (he had been in hiding since the arrest of Notaras, when the police had just barely missed him) at a certain place at 10:15 P.M. A lady friend of mine volunteered to come in her car at 10:00 and park about one hundred yards from where I was staying. We knew that at 9:00 the porter of the block of flats I was staying in left his stand and retired to his apartment. So I was given keys to both the flat and the main entrance and cautiously went out wearing eyeglasses, which I don't usually do. I went to the corner of the street; my friend had just arrived in her car. I hopped in and she took me straight to the meeting place. But Vassilis was not there! We circled about for a while, and ten minutes later I saw Vassilis's form (he is a big athletic man, then in his early forties). I got out and we took a walk, talking away, while my vigilant friend parked her car nearby and watched. In fifteen minutes we had said all we had to, and I watched him get into an old black Citroën and vanish in the darkness. I then walked back to my friend's car, and she returned me to my hideout. She had the nerve to pass under the very nose of a military tank in Ambelokipi Square. The whole operation took about thirty-five minutes. I cannot disclose her name but want her to know of my gratitude for this, and two other, more dangerous, matters she helped me with, during that first year of the dictatorship.

A funny incident happened while I was in hiding. The gentleman in whose house I was staying was having his name day—we celebrate namedays, not birthdays, in Greece—and we decided that it would be good camouflage if the couple held a little party for their friends, as they were in the habit of doing at that time of year. The party was to start at 8:00 P.M. There were about twenty guests. So I was duly locked up in a very small storeroom with a chair and a book; we thought that if the room I slept in (the guest bedroom of the four-room apartment) was locked, it might appear suspicious to some of the guests. Sure enough, I was told the next day that three ladies in turn had gone into the room and used it and its mirror, to put on a little lipstick and comb their hair. The party lasted until 2:00 in the morning! When the last guest had left, my hosts opened my "prison" and helped me to all sorts of wonderful food they had been enjoying throughout the evening.

Christmas came, and it was announced that the Junta was granting a partial amnesty, so to speak. A number of political figures were set free. By the description of the people it affected, I saw that I obviously would have been one of them; so I left my hiding place on Christmas Eve and went home. At that time Andreas Papandreou was also released from prison. He had been in prison all through the period following April 21.

His father, the elder Papandreou, our leader, had remained in prison for about two months, and then had been detained under house arrest.

In September 1967 the house arrest was partially lifted for a short period. A guard remained outside, but Papandreou could receive visitors. It was then I visited him. I saw him again for the last time in January 1968, after the King's counter-coup, when the partial amnesty was granted.

In both these meetings, George Papandreou was serene, sad, and yet optimistic that in the end democracy would prevail in Greece. The first thing he said when I entered the second-floor bedroom of his house in Kastri the morning his house arrest was lifted was, "My boy"—I was one of his youngest ministers—"I never thought they would have dared." And I believe he was sincere. He expressed his uneasiness about the fate of his son* and twice said he regretted he had ever urged him to return to Greece. It was then he asked me to see what I could do by clandestinely getting out of the country to inform western Europe of the plight of Greece. He said he would enrust the task of representing the party abroad to a three-member committee: former ministers George Mavros, Athanassios Kanellopoulos, and myself, since we were all well-educated men, spoke foreign languages fluently, and represented the spectrum of the tendencies in the party. This plan did not materialise before the King's counter-coup, although I exchanged views on its implementation with the others.

My second and last meeting with George Papandreou took place at his home in late January of 1968. He was tired and dispirited after the failure of the King's coup, but happy that his son Andreas had been released and permitted to leave the country. "I'm sure he'll do a good job abroad," he said.

* He was still in prison then: September 1967.

"The committee will no longer be necessary." He then turned to internal resistance, praised me for my participation in it, and gave me a very precious piece of advice. "Use unknown people," he said. "Avoid public figures for the real work. They will be suspected, followed, and arrested sooner or later." He kissed me on my forehead and wished me good luck. Within a few months I had been arrested and he was dead.

I met Andreas Papandreou for a few minutes once after his release, in late December of 1967. We agreed on the details of a second meeting—(I had a number of important things to tell him)—but he never turned up. A few days later he managed to get a passport and leave Greece, after much American pressure had been put on the Junta.

It was in late February or early March of 1968 that I was first called to the Athens Security Police and confronted by the notorious Lambrou, who had already made quite a sorry name for himself as a torturer. A policeman came to my home very early one morning—that was part of the intimidation technique—and said I should report to the Athens Security on Bouboulinas Street within a day. I knew that that did not mean arrest, for the time being at least, because people under arrest were never given notice beforehand; otherwise they could manage to go into hiding or escape. A bit later in the day I heard that a number of other Centre Union members of Parliament had also been summoned. I decided it was best to go; it would show I had nothing to hide. Later I found out that, at that time, they were not clearly aware of my Democratic Defence activities anyway.

Basil Lambrou,* Vice-Chief of the Athens Security Police,

* He is a relative of the Chief of the Armed Forces under the Junta, General Angelis, who is known for his close association with the American Pentagon. After the decision of the Council of Europe, in which Lambrou was mentioned in person as a torturer, he was transferred to another service. Of course, other torturers continue the work in his place.

was a man of about fifty, well-built, wearing a dark blue suit, and respectable-looking at first glance. He received me in a small office with a huge picture of the dictator Papadopoulos over his head. He asked me to sit and he even offered coffee, which I declined.

"I would like to ask you a few questions," he said, "concerning the political situation."

Detecting a trap, I answered, "Politicians make statements in Parliament or the press, not at police headquarters."

He was taken aback, and an ugly look came to his face. "Why, is this place not important enough for you? Do you despise a civil employee for doing his duty?"

"I have been to this building before, Mr. Lambrou, but as the lawyer of a criminal; and I respected the men of the police for doing their duty. Today I am asked to discuss politics with you, which, according to Papadopoulos, is illegal anyway. I am not prepared to."

"You are not cooperative, and you have completely misunderstood me. I just wanted to ask you who the chief of your party is."

"George Papandreou; everyone knows that," I answered.

"Not Andreas?" he said. "You know," he went on, "that Andreas Papandreou has taken an anti-national attitude abroad. Do you approve of that?"

"I am not aware of any anti-national statement of Andreas," I said. "What are you referring to?"

Lambrou produced a copy of the fascist paper, *Eleftheros Kosmos,* and showed me the editorial, written by the known Junta agent Savvas Konstandopoulos, which included all sorts of insults aimed at Andreas.

"That's not a statement by Andreas," I said, "it's a statement by his opponents you are showing me."

"You know, you are being a little difficult. Perhaps it's your age." Then he changed the subject. "So Andreas is not your leader. I think you should just write down the fact that you do not adhere to Andreas as your leader, and that will be the end of it."

"I'm sorry, but I will not write or make any political statement under the circumstances."

At that moment he was interrupted by the telephone. When he finished he unexpectedly said, "Mr. Minister, I think that will be all." And he led me to the elevator. Walking down the corridor and pointing to the walls of the building that badly needed repair, he remarked, "The Security must acquire a new building; this one is too old."

"I hope the day will come when it will not need a building at all," I answered.

"That will happen only if the Republic of Plato is established." This is an ordinary expression in Greek meaning a dream that will never come true. "In your interest I hope not to see you here again," he added, and said goodbye.

That was the general tone of the conversation. It was obvious that he was still under orders to keep it cool with the political men of the parliamentary régime. I did hear a few days later that he told an acquaintance of mine: "With some of my visitors [referring to the members of Parliament who had been called in] we'll have trouble, and I can tell you two: Mylonas and Alevras."

It was in late March and April of 1968 that I was again called in, twice, this time by the Commander of the Security of the Athens suburbs, Colonel Karabatsos. He told me rather bluntly that he had information that I was "not keeping quiet," and that if I did not stop my anti-government activities I would be arrested. I asked what activities he was referring to, but got no answer. Seeing that he was fishing and did not have any hard facts against me, I insisted that he name my activities so that I could offer an explanation. He did not. He was vague and threatening. I said I had done nothing illegal and was ready to answer any accusation. He then backed up a little and told me to be sure and behave, as if I were a schoolboy. I smiled. Quite annoyed, he asked me to leave.

The second time I was called in to headquarters I did not see him. After waiting for about two hours, I was told that I had been called in by mistake. Supposedly some secretary had not noted that I had answered the first call. It was the usual intimidation technique.

I felt that they were gradually closing in on me and that my arrest would only be a matter of time. I doubled my precautions. By this time, May 1968, my house was being watched by plainclothesmen on a twenty-four-hour basis, and I was followed about everywhere I went. Still, I intensified my resistance work. By the early summer, Vassilis Filias and a group of other Democratic Defence fighters had been arrested in Athens. Again I was lucky. He was arrested half an hour before he was due for an appointment with me and another man. It was not a success for the Athens security forces; we had managed to dodge them up to that time. Someone bringing a message to us from the Salonica Democratic Defence was trailed to his meeting with Filias.

I have since come to know that it was in Salonica that my name as a leading member of Democratic Defence first surfaced. But they avoided arresting me for about three months in the hope that they would get others by trailing me. Fortunately, they didn't get anything.

The decision to arrest me was taken in July 1968 and was only delayed for lack of the right opportunity. It was decided not to bring me to public trial under any circumstances because it would hurt the image of the new government. Exiling me to a forlorn island where I could be conveniently forgotten was more practical. Modern dictatorships are skillful in building face-saving techniques. A month later, after I had done my best to reorganise the Board of Democratic Defence, I was arrested on August 14, 1968, the day Alexander Panagoulis* made an attempt on the life of Papadopoulos, an attempt in which Democratic Defence and the other men who were arrested that night and brought to the Maroussi jail were not implicated.

* He tried to blow up Papadopoulos's car but had failed. Panagoulis has since, through his immense suffering at the hands of the torturers of the Military Police, become a symbol of resistance to the hated dictatorship.

4

CONTROLLING AN EXILE

During my exile I managed to keep a short diary of things that happened every day, written in an inoffensive way and without mentioning names, so that nobody would be incriminated if the diary were found. I did not take it with me on my escape. I had it smuggled out three months before I left.

I used to wake up at about 7:30, prepare myself a little breakfast, and present myself to the police at 9:00. I would sign the register and then return home and start reading. The number of books I read was considerable: historical works, in most cases, political and Greek history. I read quite a bit of ancient Greek literature and foreign literature, too. At noon I would have my lunch at Mrs. Aspasia's tavern and afterward resume my reading. At 6:00 I would present myself at the police station again and return to go to bed rather early. I never went out to the tavern for my evening meal. I started staying home for reasons of health. In the end, the fact that I did not appear in the evening at the tavern played a part in my escape plan. I always took about an hour's walk in the morning in the winter and in the late afternoon during the summer.

Every evening after the night really set in, two armed gendarmes would arrive outside my house and remain until the sun rose next morning. The guards changed at midnight. I checked on that to make sure they weren't just placing someone there at the beginning of the night and early in the morning to give me the impression that I was being guarded all through the night. By getting up in the middle of the night, walking very slowly in my bare feet, going out on the terrace that was on the top of my house, and looking down, I discovered that guards were there at any time of night and in any weather. It was clear that the night was certainly not the time to escape, if an escape was ever to take place; and the idea of escaping got into my head soon after I reached Amorgos.

During the day matters were easier. There were always two policemen on duty, one in the morning and one in the afternoon. It was their job to know exactly where I was, all the time. But that wasn't done too obviously. The policeman used to follow me at a distance and generally know where I was. He would come nearer and actually walk behind me, or at my side, only on special occasions (when there was a tourist in the village, a ceremony, or during the arrival or departure of another exile).

Very quickly the question of my walks came up. After my heart attack in 1967, the doctor had advised me to do a lot of walking, not very quick walking, but a lot. I was a walker before that anyway, and I like to go about in the country. I told the gendarmerie chief that I didn't think that the order about my not leaving the boundaries of the village meant that I couldn't go beyond the last house in the village. I said I was sure it meant the boundaries of the local community of Hora, which included all the fields, rocks, and little hills around the village. His view was rather a different one, but after I explained that I didn't want to walk just for fun but that it was part of my health regimen, he agreed that I could go out beyond the village—but never far. And that gradually became a routine. In the meanwhile Polychronopoulos was replaced by another sergeant, Pericles Palaiologopoulos, who gradually accepted the same arrangement. I myself was rather surprised by it: when I used to walk through the village streets, I was followed about, but when I left the village—and escape became possible—I was not. The policeman on duty used to follow me toward the exit from the village I had chosen to take that day for my walk, walk a few yards outside the village, and then sit on a stone and wait for my return.

Was it laziness? I didn't know. I soon found out that it was a principle, because all the policemen on duty did the same thing. Perhaps it was a sort of face-saving technique; if I were seen walking along those little country paths outside the village with a policeman at my heels, their surveillance perhaps became too obvious. The idea of the deportation or exile system is supposed to be that you are obliged to live normally in another place. It is meaningless, however, to try and interpret laws under a dictatorship, even the dictator's own laws. So I started my little walks. There were obviously some moments when I was not seen by the gendarme on duty. I always returned quickly and gave the impression of following a daily routine.

There were three shops in the village that sold practically everything, from food to copybooks and pencils, and poor quality fabrics. Therefore I had an excuse to enter one of these shops practically every day. There was always something I wanted to buy: envelopes, canned food or matches, a cup and saucer, or a piece of string. I quickly became friendly with the shopkeepers. The policeman rarely entered the shop with me. He used to walk outside, so I always had time for a little conversation with the shopkeepers. All three happened to belong to the Right, but they were earnestly opposed to the dictatorship, as was practically everyone else in Hora. There was also a baker, two cobblers, three cafés, a greengrocer, and some other shops. As a result, I managed to become informed about things: details like, "Such and such a policeman will be going on leave in a few days" (overheard the previous night at the tavern) or, "They were on a sort of special mission yesterday on that side of the island"—all sorts of information. Another friend, whose house was strategically located not far from mine, gave me a good deal of information about the way I was being followed and guarded. There were many similar cases which I will not mention, because I have to think of the safety of these people. It all came quite naturally to them, and they certainly proved worthy of my confidence.

Another interesting figure was the midwife. She was a woman of about seventy, still going strong. I met her one day on the narrow little central street of Hora, which had been grandly named "21st of April Avenue" by the dictatorship (the small central square of the village was called "Square of the Christian Greeks" after one of the slogans of the dictatorship). As I was strolling down 21st of April Avenue, this woman was coming up, and as she passed by me she whispered, "I can take blood pressure, too." I didn't immediately grasp what it was about. But then I remembered she was the midwife of the village, and I understood that this meant that I could go and see her without appearing to disobey the order against entering private houses. I could say I went because I wanted my blood pressure taken. I had heard that she was a good woman, and I asked one of the grocers what he thought of her. The grocer, who was a conservative man of the Right but a believer in democratic procedures, answered me, "She's all right, she's with us; she's a leftist." This answer from a rightist would have been unthinkable before the dictatorship. When I later went and met the midwife, I purposely asked her, "What sort of man is the grocer?"

"Oh," she said, "he's a black rightist. But you can have confidence in him, he's all right; we are together now."

Dictator Papadopoulos has repeatedly said that he has united the country. He certainly has! The Colonels have become the common enemy against whom the Greek people united, regardless of their views on the social structure of post-Junta Greece. This *de facto* creation of conditions of political alliance among all the political camps is an event of great importance. Duly developed, it can lead to the quicker liberation of the country and greatly facilitate the smooth functioning of democratic institutions after the overthrow of the dictatorship. And to think that all this is due to the Junta! The ancient Greeks were right in saying that anything bad had a portion of good in it.

So the next day I went to the midwife's house. The policeman who happened to be near me—he was one of the more polite ones—said, "But where are you going?"

"To have my blood pressure taken by the midwife," I replied.

"All right," he said, as if confirming that this was a public place where one could go. (Of course, he duly reported it to his chief, who asked me about it when I went to sign in in the afternoon.) I knocked at her door and went into the house. When she had closed the door she immediately embraced me and said, "My boy, we're with you; what do you want from us?"

"There might be a few things," I said.

I sat down and she offered me sweets.

"Let's start by taking the blood pressure so that we find out how much it is. When you come back again, we'll know, and can always mention the same figure if we're asked." My blood pressure proved to be 12.5, and that was the figure we always remembered. She became a good friend. I saw her from time to time, and she helped me in many ways. I will never forget dear old Madame Diamando. She is no longer in Amorgos. If she ever comes across these lines, let her know of my gratitude and forgive me for not having given the entire story. I do it in her real interest and for her protection.

The attitude of the villagers toward me was touching. It was quite a poor village. They didn't have too much food, and often, when ships didn't come in, they actually lacked certain essential food items. The products of the island were scarce. Yet hardly a day went by when I went out for my walk that the villagers didn't take the occasion to leave me—in plates, in pieces of paper, in bags—all sorts of food: eggs, tomatoes, figs, grapes, cheese, milk. I always left the gate open. The gendarmes never bothered to guard my empty house but simply followed me about. So much food was left that I could never really use everything they sent me. Of course, I never dreamed of throwing any away or returning it; they would have been terribly offended. What is interesting is that most of the time I never knew who had left things. It was in no way a sort of give-and-take arrangement, for future, better days. I gradually found out that there were a number of people who left things for me; as a matter of fact, practically the whole village did it. The kindness of these people reached the point where they used to leave eggs for me at a time when there was a great shortage of eggs in the village. Hens don't lay all the year round, and often the ship bringing eggs didn't come in. Yet I always found a few eggs among the other items they were kind enough to leave for me. For health reasons, I rarely eat eggs. In the end I had so many I sent a large package of them to my two granddaughters. (The eldest, Alexandra, was very nearly three when I was arrested; she is now seven. The other, Christina, was born while I was in Amorgos; she is now over four, and I have never seen her.)

Another interesting character in Amorgos was the barber, Marcos, who opened his little shop once a week, or once every fortnight on Saturdays. He gave haircuts to the villagers, and I think he used to cut the wool of the lambs, too. His shop was very small. Only one chair could fit in it, together with a mirror in front. If it was not raining, the other customers waited outside in the square. Marcos was a serious man of about forty. Unlike most barbers, he spoke very little, but the little he had to say was interesting and original. I learned a lot about the history and life of Amorgos. We never talked politics, and I do not know what his political leanings were. But Saturdays at Marcos's place were a diversion, and I don't think I missed a one.

Marcos was also a good fisherman. One day when he had caught two big lobsters he decided to present them to me and my co-exile, the Brigadier. He couldn't do that openly, so he took the lobsters to Mrs. Aspasia and asked her to cook them for us. When lunchtime came, I went to the tavern. A policeman was there, mainly to see that the two exiles sitting at lunch would not speak to each other. That day I sat at my little table, the Brigadier sat on the other side of the room— we nodded to each other—and the policeman sat somewhere in the middle. Out came Mrs. Aspasia from her kitchen.

"Gentlemen," she said, "today I have something very good —lobster—but it's going to be a bit expensive. You'll have to pay more than usual. Will you have it?" She said this in a very public way, but as she approached the table to put the plate before me, she added, "Of course, you won't pay anything. It is a gift from Marcos, but I have to go through this little act so that the policeman hears it."

I and my friend the Brigadier answered that we certainly would pay a little more. Our menu was different that day!

Every day I took my walks. They were very lonely walks: myself, my thoughts, and nature. I enjoyed them. The contact with both flora and fauna appeals to me greatly. Often I would sit on a stone and watch a donkey grazing. He would soon stop, and we would look each other understandingly in the eyes for minutes on end.

Sometimes during these walks I would meet villagers who had gone out to their fields and, since the policeman remained quite far behind and out of sight, I would take the occasion to speak to them. There wasn't one who favoured the dictatorship. There was no pretense; they weren't merely trying to be nice. You could see how fiercely they hated the idea of a dictatorship and the lack of liberty in the country. They used to give me news—many times exaggerated, of course, because under a dictatorship rumours thrive—about what was going on in Athens and stories about scandals of the dictatorship. And they gave me all the information they had about the doings of the policemen in Amorgos. I made friends that way with a number of people.

A ship came to the island once a week in winter; sometimes, when there was very bad weather, it came only every ten to fifteen or even twenty days. In summer there was a ship two or three times a week, which brought the mail. I was rather surprised to find out after a while that the censorship of my letters had not already taken place at the headquarters of the Security in Athens; it was simply carried out at Hora by the gendarmerie sergeant who headed the six-man detachment guarding me. There was a post office in my village, located in a very old house—the date 1797 is inscribed on it. The post office consists of one large room with two tables. On one side of the table sits the man who takes care of everything having to do with the post; he sells stamps, takes letters, and gives out mail. On the other side, an employee sits who deals with anything that has to do with telegrams and telephones. Amorgos has a telegraph system and just one single nonautomatic telephone. The telephone rings in that very room, and there's a small enclosure for private conversations. There is also a second line to Gendarmerie Headquarters. The other eight villages on Amorgos are connected with the outside world by local telephone through Hora.

One day, as I was taking my walk, I was surprised by an old couple, husband and wife, who were returning from the fields. They hid behind a rock and some bushes and made a sign to me. I went over and sat beside them near a tree. The old woman did most of the talking. "We are with you, Mr. Mylonas," she said, "and we think we should tell you a few things so that you are aware of what's going on and will know how to take the proper precautions. Don't ask how we have found out, but you can be sure that through a very roundabout way we have found out exactly how the whole system works. We'll start by telling you today, but you shouldn't stay too long. The policeman might become suspicious. But we will gradually give you the whole story."

It took four meetings, spread out over two weeks, before they had finished.

"Here's the situation. When the ship comes in the letters are brought to the post office by car at about 9:00 A.M. The whole bag of letters is then sorted out. Any letters addressed to you or the Brigadier are put aside. A little later, a policeman goes to the post office; he always carries a green bag. He takes the letters, puts them in the bag so that they're not seen by anyone outside, and returns to the police station. There the letters are opened through the old familiar process of boiling water in a kettle; the steam moistens the envelope so it can easily be opened and later restuck. The letters are read by the gendarmerie sergeant, who usually returns them to the postman by the afternoon of the same day. So there's no point in going to the post office to pick up a letter before the end of the day on which the ship arrives.

"However," they continued—and I suppose this had already

brought us to our second session, because they relayed little bits of information each time—"if the letter is not returned to the post office by closing time of the day the ship has arrived, it is returned instead to the postman a day or two later. He is under orders from the Gendarmerie to withhold that letter until the day another ship arrives."

"Are you sure?" I asked.

"Positive," the old man said.

There were two questions I had. First of all, could the dictatorship possibly think that I imagined there was no censorship? Perhaps the police wanted me to think censorship took place before letters arrived. Second, why didn't they keep the letters at the Gendarmerie Headquarters until the day the postman could hand them to me? After all, the postman might very well give them to me earlier than he should. Obviously, he enjoyed their confidence. But even if he didn't there could be serious consequences for him if he were asked by the sergeant to produce the letters before the arrival of the next ship and he didn't have them.

As the weeks and months went by, I noticed that 10-15 percent of my letters were withheld in the manner described. Four or five times the old lady actually managed to show these delayed letters to me so that I could find out who they were from and what their contents were. Once there was a letter I was very eager to read because I knew it contained some coded information. So I asked her, "Could I read that letter?"

She looked up toward heaven and then said, "I will help you, but please do the following. I'll give you this letter now. Put it very deep in your pocket, take it home, open it through the kettle technique, read it, and then bring it back to me as quickly as you can. The postman will hand it to you officially the day the ship arrives without being any the wiser." I took the letter home, opened it with the steam system, read it, was very glad I had, and a little while later took it back to the old lady (I cannot say where or how).

"Be quite sure you don't answer this letter," she said, "because then the police will know you have read it."

I was very careful to follow her advice; I naturally wanted to keep the association going, and I didn't wish to harm these invaluable friends.

But that was done only once. I didn't get very many letters anyway. The ones that came were mainly from my family and from a few friends. Many other people were afraid to write to me because it could get them into trouble. Sometimes I would receive a letter signed with a pseudonym and I would have to figure out who it was from.

Most of my letters were received regularly on the afternoon of the day the ship arrived. Some were withheld for a while and I would get them later. But there were some letters that were very late arriving. I think the record was held by one from Athens that took seventy-two days to reach my hands. Obviously, these were letters that included something that made the authorities suspicious. The sergeant must have thought he detected some secret in them that went beyond his authority to handle, and he would post them back to Athens to his superiors. The record-breaking letter was of no political importance at all: it was a family letter from my daughter Maria. Another which took about sixty days to reach me, was a simple card from a former minister and member of Parliament of the Centre Union, George Mavros, who acknowledged my condolences on the death of his mother-in-law. Probably most of the mail that was sent to me actually reached me in the end, but it was always a matter of time, and time, of course, is important if you are to rely on correspondence. But could I have confidence in letters that conveyed coded information, since I had no way of knowing whether they would be given to me in a day's time or in seventy days' time? That more or less excluded using letters for anything urgent, anything having to do with plans for my escape. I always made sure to post outgoing letters at least twenty-four hours before the ship came, so that they could be censored and sent on time. I calculated that there again I missed a ship now and then.

Sometimes certain letters of the villagers also came under this censorship system. The post office would get the order from the Gendarmerie to keep the letters of X, Y, and Z and turn them in for censorship. This would last for about a month or so, and then the order would be rescinded. It was a very good way of finding out which people they suspected, who might be considered a friend of mine, who might be thought to be helping me through his mail to write things that I could not write, and so forth. By acquiring this information, I was always sure of what my standing was with the Gendarmerie. I must say that a number of times they actually did hit on the people that were closer to me than others, and that made us doubly careful.

The other means of communication was through telegrams. I received very few and I don't think I sent a single one. Telegrams, being infrequent in the village, were always censored. Mine were under a sort of special system about which I was also informed by my friends. They reported that the telecommunications man had orders that all telegrams addressed to me should be given me after a few days' time, something like a week; the idea was that if they included some coded message, it would have become completely stale by the time I got it. But my defence system was easy. When the telegram arrived, my friends would inform me of its contents. It would be duly kept for a number of days and officially given to me later. But all the same it was unsound to rely on telegrams for any important and quick communication, anything related to my escape, for example. I could not be sure that my counter-espionage system would always work. Suppose the post-office men or the police found out? And what if the old couple got into trouble? I repeatedly thanked them warmly for their courageous help and more than once asked them to discontinue it. They were stubbornly human and democratic. "It's the least we can do for you," they said.

From the beginning I was greatly puzzled over how their ingenious work was done, but I didn't like to ask my kind friends too many questions. I did find out something about it, however, toward the end of my stay in Amorgos. The old man was taken to the hospital in Piraeus, and then his wife confided in me on one of my evening walks that love played an important role in the plan. Fortunately, circumstances permit me at this time to tell the story without hurting anyone. The beautiful and intelligent niece of the postman was having a love affair with the old couples' grandson, a seaman. It was she who helped clean the post office every afternoon after her uncle went home. She would secretly gather all this information and then relay it to her fiancé. An ardent democrat, he in turn transmitted everything to his grandparents. The young people are now married and living in the United States. We have since exchanged letters and I have received their permission to publish this story. The grandfather, bless his soul, died a year later. The old lady is no longer in Amorgos. I'm sure that if she ever reads these lines she will be proud of herself and ready to face any ill-doings of the Junta.

There were other methods of communication. One was the telephone, which I was told I could use only on special occasions, and only for family business. I used the telephone sparingly, I suppose five or six times in all during the year and two months I remained in Hora. I did receive a few phone calls. My brother-in-law called me about two months after I was sent into exile on a purely business matter. I had been his lawyer for years, and he wanted to check up on a few things regarding a case another lawyer was handling for him. We exchanged a few good words at the end, and that was all. The day after, as I heard later, he was summoned by the Security Police and asked why he had communicated over the telephone with an exile. He bears another name and the police were not aware of our relationship. He was very strictly reprimanded and told that he should never do such a thing again; it had become part of his record, and from that moment on he would be considered a suspicious person. When he explained that he was just my brother-in-law, they did seem to be somewhat placated, but he was still told that he'd better avoid such contacts if he didn't want to get into trouble.

The procedure for telephone calls was simple. I would get a written message from the post office, say at 8:00 A.M., saying, "You have a telephone call coming in at 11:00." A copy of the message would be given to the police, and the moment I entered the telephone booth at the post office, my line would be connected to the Gendarmerie so that they could listen too. But at least there was the great advantage of immediacy. Provided we had agreed on a code for different things, we could talk right under the nose of the police and be satisfied that the message had been transmitted. This is the system that was finally used by me twice in the days nearing my escape.

The fourth system of communication was sending letters through messengers. Usually I never met them personally. Friends in the village would give letters to a relative who was leaving for Piraeus. When the relative arrived in Athens, he would get the letter delivered to my home somehow. He would never post it within Athens, because letters addressed to my family were also censored. Rather, the messengers were asked to take the letter to some specific place, and from there it would ultimately reach my family.

There was, finally, a fifth method of communicating with the outside world. In most Greek islands there's the system of the so-called private postman. These are men who make the trip back and forth to Piraeus carrying parcels to and from friends and relatives; you give them a few drachmas for that. It's an old system that still survives in these villages, and these postmen—there were two who came and went at times from Amorgos—could be made use of. However, I was warned that neither of them was sure politically, and you could never be certain what they would say because they wanted to be okay with the police. Once I used one of them quite officially. I told the police that I would like to send my family a few odd books and things I did not need anymore through this unofficial postman, and they said it would be all right. I never found out if they actually opened the parcel or not. But what I could do was to include something of mine in a parcel being sent by other villagers to Athens or Piraeus. I made use of this system once. But shortly after, an announcement was made that all parcels carried by private postmen would be opened by the police before they left, and that the postman would have to sign a statement saying that he was aware that nothing illegal was included in the parcels he took. So that was the end of that system for me.

My relationship with my fellow exile was a rather odd one. We usually exchanged a few words in the presence of the policeman while having lunch at Aspasia's place, and we also met at police headquarters when we came to sign in twice a day. One day I was reprimanded quite strictly by the sergeant.

"You talked to the Brigadier," he said. "You know it is forbidden. Why do you do it?"

I was so surprised that I really thought someone had falsely denounced us, reporting that we had been seen talking at length somewhere, which was not the case. So I said, "No, I don't. I never do. I think it's stupid that I am forbidden to, but it just hasn't happened. The only conversation I have with him is to exchange a few words from one end of the tavern to the other while we are sitting at separate tables and eating, in the presence of the policeman, saying something about the weather or asking him how he slept or how he felt, and he asking me about my children and so forth."

"Well, that's exactly what I refer to," said the gendarmerie segreant. He certainly was applying the letter of the law.

Of course, when the time really came for me to communicate with the Brigadier, I did manage to meet him for about five minutes in complete privacy. This was arranged through the friendly auspices of one of the villagers in a roundabout way. I will mention it here, although it's related to my escape.

I went to the shop of this villager and, while buying something, I said, "I must see the Brigadier."

He calmly answered, "I'll arrange it, and I'll let you know."

Two days later as I was passing outside his shop, he called me, "Mr. Mylonas, I have those potatoes you asked for."

I had ordered no potatoes, but I understood that this was a signal. I went in, he handed me a few potatoes to take home, and at the same time told me, "Tomorrow at eleven at the church of St. Titus. Are you sure you know where it is?"

I said I did.

"As you enter the church, light a candle," he added.

I thanked him and left.

That afternoon I made my first visit to the area and saw how intelligent the man had been. The church of St. Titus, a little whitewashed church of the fifteenth or sixteenth century, is very small. It is located in a narrow street that is shaped like a corkscrew. If you walk up the street and are followed, you can enter the church before the policeman, trailing at least fifty metres behind, has a chance to see you. He'll most likely go by the church, thinking he's following you through the corkscrew to the end of the street. Since this street ends very near where my house was, the policeman might easily think that I had gone home.

The next day, a little before 11:00, I was in the village square. The policeman was hanging around, and I started into the corkscrew street as if going back home. I don't even think he bothered to follow me; he was more or less sure I was going home. He probably thought that he would pick up my traces a little later, perhaps at the tavern when I had lunch. At exactly 11:00 I opened the door of the church and went in. It was very dark. I lit a candle. That was the signal to the Brigadier, who was in the church already, hiding behind the altar. Immediately I heard a voice—quite impressive in the darkness.

"I'm here. What do you want, my friend?"

I quickly went into my story. "I'm preparing to escape. Are you interested in joining me?"

I must say here that I informed no one at all in the village of my plan of escape, purely for security reasons. I was not afraid they would give me away, but they might talk about it at home, and also it could cause trouble for them after I had departed. If they didn't know anything, the police wouldn't be able to get anything out of them. But I believed it was my duty, as a man, to inform my fellow exile and ask him to join me if he wanted to.

The Brigadier emerged from behind the altar, took my hands in his and said, "I'll never forget this, thank you."

He said he would think it over and give me his answer later. He had the time to tell me that he thought it was a very dangerous proposition, that he didn't think it could succeed, and that I would be endangering my life.

"Don't forget Mandilaras,"* he added.

He answered me later with a little note. As I was going by a store, I was called in for some item that had supposedly just arrived and that I might be interested in buying—some sort of canned food, I think.

The storekeeper handed me a box of these cans. Under them

* Nikiforos Mandilaras, a well-known Athenian lawyer who was shot and killed while trying to escape abroad in the first weeks of the dictatorship. His body was found mutilated in the sea near the island of Rhodes.

I found a little note in a sealed envelope in the handwriting of the Brigadier. He said he had thought it over and that it was impossible for him to come along because of his health condition. It was only then that I learned that he had but one kidney and that his health was too precarious for him to embark on such an undertaking. As a matter of fact, he wrote that he had already submitted a petition asking to be transferred to another place where he would be near a hospital in case of danger.

Well, that took care of that, and it certainly simplified matters. I was pleased that I had told him and behaved the way I had. On the other hand, I was relieved that he didn't accept my offer, because it would have been more difficult for two to escape than one. He was later transferred to a mountainous village near Tripolis in the Peloponnesus where there was a hospital. I have since heard that he was later released, re-arrested, and, I think, released again in poor health.

For three months, there was no other exile on the island. Then, in May 1969, another exile arrived, Squadron Commander Diakoumatos, who had been with me in that Maroussi jail. That posed another problem for me. With my program of escape beginning to take shape by then, I had to inform him, too. With him it was simpler. I didn't go through an elaborate stratagem to meet him; I was able to get it done more directly. We used to pass each other every day in the village. I knew he spoke good English, so whenever I met him, as if saying good morning or good evening, I would give him a little bit of a sentence—which our respective policemen, being at a distance, could not overhear. I'd say something like: "I am planning to escape from here. Are you interested?"

The next day he asked, "How and when?"

After four or five meetings, I got the message across. There again, I was pleased that I had done so and, I will admit, also pleased that there was a negative answer.

"I'm no politician," said the airman. "What will I do if I go abroad? You will carry on the fight. I think I'm better here; there's always a chance I will be released and can fight the dictatorship within the country."

I remember his saying very well, "You will never be released," which was a correct assessment of the situation, I think. He was a much younger man than I, about thirty-five. He told me that his wife was pregnant with their first child, and he just couldn't see himself leaving. So that took care of that. The Brigadier and the Squadron Commander were both serious people and I was sure I was undergoing no risks when I told them my secret. I didn't give them any details; I never had the time to. In any case, the details were far from laid out when I spoke to them.

There was no hospital in Amorgos. There was a doctor, a rural doctor as we call them in Greece, appointed by the state to visit the villages of a certain area. The doctor on the island of Amorgos made the rounds of the eight villages and once in a while would be in my village. Some of the villagers told me that they didn't think he was much; I never actually had anything to do with him. My prescriptions and medicines were sent from Athens and, of course, I never had any blood tests or cardiograms during my fourteen-month stay on the island, although I was supposed to have one every month. I was not personally mistreated by the dictatorship in the way so many others were, but even my case shows how little they cared about one's life: if I had had a serious heart attack on Amorgos, that would have been the end of me. They certainly knew of my ailment.

I had only one occasion to see the doctor. One day, as I was having my lunch and eating an olive, I somehow broke a tooth on the pit. Part of the tooth fell off. A little later, I found myself with a bad toothache and soon my right cheek was all swollen. I went to the sergeant, showed it to him, and said, "I want permission to be taken to a nearby island, one on which there is a dentist, so that I can be treated." Of course, I would be followed by one or two gendarmes to the place and brought back.

"Yes, that can be done," he said, "but I can't order it. You'll have to submit a petition, which I will send to my superiors back in Athens, and they will have to okay it."

I didn't exactly relish the prospect of waiting with a toothache for a month or two, or however long it took to get an answer. Naxos, the island I thought I could go to, was about three or four hours away by ship, and the matter could be taken care of in a few days. I therefore wrote out the petition and took it to him.

"I want a medical certificate attached proving that you are ill," the sergeant said.

"What do you need the certificate for? You see me with your own eyes. I'm all swollen."

"Ah yes, but orders are orders. Go to the doctor and he'll give you a certificate that will prove that you are in need of medical care."

I went to the doctor, but he was not there. I was told he was away and that he wouldn't be back for a fortnight. When I returned to the Gendarmerie and explained that the doctor was away, the sergeant lifted his hands in helplessness. "I can't do anything about it," he said.

Following the advice of villagers, I used camomile to reduce the pain. A few days later the doctor returned.

He was one of the few men on the island who was a follower of the dictatorship. But, contrary to what one would have expected, that made him servile toward me.

"Mr. Minister, we're honoured by your visit at our medical office."

I asked for a certificate saying I needed to go to a dentist. He said he would be glad to give me one, but it would take time and I would have to put up with the toothache while I was waiting for clearance.

"Couldn't you cure my tooth then?" I asked.

He wasn't supposed to. He was a general practitioner. The only thing he could do was to pull it out. I said, "Do so," and sat in his chair while he extracted my tooth. There was a nurse there, too, Aphroditi, a very kind woman. She spoke little, but somehow, catching her eye, I felt she was no admirer of Papadopoulos.

One day I was at the tavern of Mrs. Aspasia, as usual, having my *plat du jour*, lentils perhaps or marrows, when I saw a group of tourists, two ladies and a gentleman, having their meal. They were speaking French. Tourists did come through this rather forlorn village in summer, not in great numbers, perhaps one hundred of them throughout the summer. About an hour's walk from the village there was a very interesting Byzantine monastery; it had been built on a steep hill overlooking the sea in the year 1088 by the Emperor Alexios Komninos, and tourists would pass through my village on their way to see this monastery, usually on donkey or on foot. I visited it myself, after having asked permission and with an escort of two policemen.

As I sat in my lonely corner of the tavern, suddenly one of the two ladies, not looking at me at all, but looking at one of her friends, lifted her glass and made a toast. I heard her say in French, "We know who you are; we hope you will soon be set free and that democracy will return to your country."

Then the man raised his glass and, as if they were celebrating a birthday or anniversary, he looked the woman in the eyes and answered along the same lines: wishes for the good of democracy in our country and so on. That was the end of it. The gendarme, of course, understood nothing. I suppose my unknown friends were not sure if I had understood either, since they didn't know if I spoke French. I was moved by their kindness and wanted to get some message through to thank them. After lunch the gendarme stepped outside, so as I was walking out of the tavern I turned towards them and said in French, "I heard you. Goodbye, and thank you with all my heart."

It's a little story, perhaps unimpressive, but things like that can be very important to a lonely exile. I'm a gregarious person and, at the same time, I must have some sort of solitary monk's qualities in me. I can live alone for long spells, especially when I read and write. I didn't write much, not knowing what the fate of any text might be. But I studied and thought about all that had led to the dictatorship.

5
THE YEARS I WAS YOUNG

I was still in Amorgos on April 6, 1969, when I reached my fiftieth birthday. I had lived half a century. That sounds like a lot of time and yet I felt I was only at the beginning. I had been born in 1919 in Paris. It was a coincidence; my parents were there because my father, Alexander Mylonas, was a member of the Greek delegation at the Versailles Conference under Premier Eleftherios Venizelos, the great Greek statesman of modern times. It so happened that my grandfather, General Panayotis Danglis, who had been the Commander-in-Chief of the Greek Army, was also there for the military part of the treaty, and my birth became quite a family affair. I spent the first three months of my life in the Paris suburb of Ville d'Avray, and then we moved back to Greece.

My grandfather Danglis died in 1924 when I was not quite five. He was a very short man, in no way a militarist, with a kind face. He had been elected three times a member of Parliament for Ioannina in Epirus, where we came from, had been Minister of Defence, and when he died he was the leader of the Liberal Party in the absence of Venizelos. He honoured freedom and democracy and counted it his duty, together with the great Venizelos and Admiral Coundouriotis, to form the Triumvirate of 1916, which dethroned the pro-German King Constantine I, brought Greece into the war on the side of the Allies, and was thus able to save great portions of Greek-inhabited territories that would otherwise have been lost.

My father was an idealist. He believed deeply in democracy and socialism. He was also repeatedly elected member of Parliament for Ioannina, and he became a cabinet minister in a number of governments, under Eleftherios Venizelos and other republican leaders. Ours was certainly a democratically oriented family in everyday life. My father and mother never once quarreled. Nor did they ever apply any strict discipline to my brother or me. I think it was their example more than anything else that educated us.

Mother is an ardent democrat; she will never give in to any totalitarian aspect of life. She's going on her eighty-sixth year now, and she is still strong. Only recently I was told that in Greece, on Christmas day, when the family was gathered round her in our house at Kiphissia, a relative drank to my health and to my quick return to Greece: my dear mother, being really true to herself, said, "I don't want him back if these gangsters are not kicked out first."

My life as a child was a happy one, what with a very warm family life and school years, which I really loved. Athens College* was part of me and has remained part of me ever since; life there was exciting and interesting. We learned many

* A Greco-American high school, considered the best school in Greece. A Greek gymnasium, or high school, corresponds to American high school, plus something like two years of junior college.

things. I will never forget among many other academic experiences the excellent system of teaching history. When I graduated in 1938, I felt that perhaps it was the end of the happiest period of my life. Most of my best friends date from those years.

I was a good student, the Valedictorian of my class, its president, the editor of the school paper and Year Book. And I was a sprinter, the holder of the college record for years. Coincidentally, my record in the 200-metre dash was broken later by my own son, Alexander.

Politics were interwoven with my life from the time of my primary school years. My father was one of the leaders of the democratic (or Venizelist, or anti-royalist) camp during the period between World Wars I and II, and I followed with ardent interest all the tribulations of Greek politics throughout those years. The Republic was proclaimed in 1924, but lasted for only eleven years. Following a coup in 1935, King George II returned to the throne.

Politics were also very much a part of our daily school life. Amazingly for teenagers, we followed every turn, every aspect, every victory and defeat of democracy, to which we were ardently devoted, in Greece and abroad. Those were the years of Hitler (whom we passionately hated), Mussolini (his poses and speeches gave us a lot of laughs), the Abyssinian campaign, and then Franco, whose successes during the terrible Spanish Civil War caused, with two or three exceptions, deep grief to all in our class. We were all for Franklin Roosevelt and the New Deal at the time.

It was in 1926 when a short-lived dictatorship under General Pangalos was overthrown in Greece—I was a boy of seven— that a friend living near our house knocked at our door at 6:00 A.M. and shouted jubilantly, "He has fallen." I still remember the excitement in the house: our love of freedom was something that never died.

In 1928, my father, then campaigning for a coming election in Ioannina, was kidnapped by brigands. Certain Greek mountains, especially in Epirus, were infested with brigands as late as 1928, and it was such a big piece of news that it made the headlines. My father was kept for three days until the ransom was paid by the government. Eleftherios Venizelos came to Ioannina, and, in a speech before a great crowd, promised that kidnappings and all the brigandage that went with them would be erased from the country during his term of office, which was just starting. And he kept his promise. We all felt it was a disgrace to Greece that such things could happen in the twentieth century. Who would have thought that forty years later the system would prosper once again throughout the lands and the skies of the world! I remember the thrill of happiness we felt when father came back home after having behaved so courageously. The place in Epirus where my father was taken by the brigands in 1928 is still called the "Mylonas Bridge" today.*

I remember the electoral victory of the rightist-royalist party (called the Populist Party) in 1933; the attack on the life of Eleftherios Venizelos and the terrible impression it made on

* My father's abduction by brigands was considered the last instance of a chronic disease that continued to plague Greek life after the shaking off of the Turkish yoke and the acquiring of national independence. The cause of this brigandage was the great poverty of the mountaineer population. The bitter political persecution under Governor Kapodistrias (1828–1831) and the first years of King Otto (1833–1843) also helped. As time went by, brigandage became a sort of "institution," with important political backing from certain reactionary government authorities. The new spirit brought to public life by Venizelos and his historic Liberal Party brought the system to an end. Speaking today, however, of the "disappearance of brigandage" in Greece becomes a figure of speech, in view of the conditions prevailing in the country. When one recalls the tortures of the dictatorship's agents and the pillage of state money by the new "Junta nobility," I believe the comparison is not to the detriment of the simpleminded, popular "brigands" of those days.

me; and, in 1935, the forceful overthrow of the republican régime by General Condylis. King George returned to the throne and a little later, when the great Venizelos died, installed a dictatorship, the second in twentieth-century Greece, under General Metaxas. My father, one of the democratic political leaders of the time, was arrested then and exiled to the island of Ikaria, where he remained for three years. My mother and brother and I were granted permission to go and visit him, and so exile was no novelty to me. Comparing his exile in Ikaria to mine in Amorgos, I noticed many similarities: a mountainous village away from the sea; extension of the deportation period from time to time; the friendly attitude of the villagers. And some differences: his movements were much freer, for example; in the evenings, we would often go to the local school teacher's home to have dinner and chat, and we would also exchange visits and take walks with other exiles who were there, things I could not dream of in Amorgos. On the other hand, my housing conditions were better, and there was no electricity in Ikaria in the late thirties.

By that time (1938) I had entered the law school of the University of Athens. My university life was far from thrilling. There was no communal life, no extra-curricular activities. The university was thronged with the agents of the Minister of Public Security. All students were obliged to enroll in the Fascist National Youth Movement (E.O.N.), which I refused to join. I told the man in charge that it was out of the question for me to be loyal to the movement since my father was an exile. It was easier than I expected. He thought a bit, and then said, "Yes, I suppose every rule can have its exception. You can go!" And I walked out, probably the only student in the entire university who was not a member of E.O.N. The second half of my four years at the university took place under the German Occupation.

I was married very young, in April 1940: I had just turned

twenty-one. Of course, it was a love affair. I went to Ikaria and asked for my father's consent. He was surprised—when he was arrested and taken away, I had been only a boy of eighteen—but he gave in. We got married and had the blessing of having three children while we were very young. I think I would be an unhappy man if I had not had children.*

On October 28, 1940, the Italians under Mussolini attacked Greece, over the Albanian border. And the miracle happened: the little nation of seven million fought back and routed the bigger country of 45 million. It was the first victory on land against the Axis. Six months of glory and rejoicing! But then on April 6, 1941, the Germans struck, too, and the Bulgarians soon joined them. The strain was too great: although we fought for two months from our northern borders down to the last beach of Crete, we were overcome. I was a private in the Greek infantry and fought in the bloody battle of Crete against the crack German paratroops. When the island finally surrendered, I was taken prisoner by the Germans. After three months spent in three consecutive prisoner-of-war camps, in Crete and Salonica, I was released to return to the "free" life of an occupied country.

Greece was occupied by the Germans, Italians, and Bulgarians. The hated Nazi swastika was raised on the Acropolis in April 1941, and by the beginning of June the entire country had been completely occupied. The Greek people entered a terrible ordeal. Greece, victorious in its war against Italian fascism, finally succumbed to the Nazis. The Hitlerite war machine fell on Greece with all its might, all its savagery, and all its treachery.

---

* A year ago at the end of a political press conference in one of the European capitals, I was asked by a magazine reporter if I could answer one nonpolitical question. I acquiesced and was asked what I considered the three most beautiful things in life. I said: "Liberty, love, and children."

When I returned to Athens after having been released from the prisoner-of-war camp, the situation was already beginning to be tense. The first great problem was famine, and by December 1941, the situation had become critical. For the first time in my life, I felt real hunger. Even in the pre-war days Greece hadn't produced enough to feed its population. With all imports closed off and the Germans requisitioning the little that was produced locally, famine struck hard. In the end, we became accustomed to it. We saw people falling dead in the streets of Athens; a municipal truck would go about to all quarters of the city with two men actually shoveling the dead into the truck. The dying children were one of the most terrible sights. It was calculated that during that winter Greece lost something like 300,000 out of a population of seven million. In late 1942, things got a little better; the belligerents agreed to permit the import of some food items into the country, under the auspices of the Red Cross.

The resistance to the enemy gradually got under way. The first act (May 1941) was to take down the German flag from the Acropolis. One of the two men who did it, Manolis Glezos, who has gone down in history as the first hero of the resistance, later joined the leftist-oriented National Liberation Front, or E.A.M. Instead of honour and fame, he faced prison and disgrace during the civil war. He was later released and elected to Parliament. Under the Junta, he was arrested and exiled for a long period.

While the occupation was dark, we all felt that victory would be on our side in the end. In a sense, the occupation was a period marked by elation and hope such as the Greeks had not experienced for years. The resistance movement spread in both the cities and the mountains. By the time Greece was liberated, nearly three-quarters of its territory had already been freed by resistance forces. I joined a cell of E.A.M. A well-known writer, the late Nikos Karvounis, was my instructor and local leader. E.A.M. finally grew to become a huge resistance organisation, and its military branch, the E.L.A.S., did great feats of arms. Unhappily, as was later proved, E.A.M.–E.L.A.S., were virtually run by diehard Communists; I say unhappily because the organisations committed a series of excesses and grave political errors.

My ideas were, and always have been, democratic and socialist—both democratic and socialist. I have always believed in democracy and I am basically convinced there is no better way of attaining any political goal than through democracy.

The four years during the period of the occupation were a new experience for the Greek people. Although they were under the worst, most repressive dictatorship they had ever known, the people really started to feel their own power. They set up local committees, they fought for their rights, they gradually entered the resistance organisations. Everyone felt that when victory came and the country was liberated, there would be a new Greece in which the people would have the ultimate voice. There was even a sort of artistic and literary renaissance under the German boot: books were published, literary circles were formed, theatre flourished. It was amazing how a new Greece seemed about to be born with the liberation of the country. Unfortunately, it did not work out that way. The first cloud came when the resistance organisations started clashing among themselves.

The Left, under Communist domination, wanted to monopolise everything. The Right, with exceptions, felt anything was all right provided the Left did not prevail. And thus, some of the more extremist groups of the Right went so far as to accept weapons from the Germans in order to fight the Left. A civil war started, mainly between E.L.A.S. (Left) on the one hand, and on the other, E.D.E.S. (Centre-Right), and a few other respectable organisations such as E.K.K.A. (Centre) and P.E.A.N. (Right). To make matters worse, the so-called

Security Battalions were founded, composed of mercenaries organised and armed by the Germans through the Quisling government. The men who joined those battalions were former criminals whose only interest was to loot, kill, violate women, and be on the strong side. Their officers were extreme-rightist elements of the disbanded Greek Army, adventurers and fanatics. A number of them are members of the present ruling Junta in Greece.

There was also the problem of the King, George II, in exile in London. The great majority of the Greek people and most of the political leaders from left to right thought that the King should not return after the war, until a plebiscite was held to decide whether Greece would remain a constitutional monarchy or become a republic. With few exceptions, everyone wanted a republic. The British, however, had confidence in King George, openly supported him, and did not wish the so-called regal question to be discussed. The possibility of a national union in favour of the republic was thus missed, and the rightist organisations under British influence gradually shifted to a pro-royalist stand. This helped to create a civil war atmosphere in occupied Greece, which part of the Communist leadership was also only too glad to encourage for their own aims.

In May 1944 a conference of all political factions was called outside Greece, in Lebanon, and my father, who had managed to escape abroad as had a number of politicians, army and naval officers, and private citizens, participated. The government of national unity, including everyone from the right to the Communist-Left, was formed under George Papandreou, and my father became the Minister of the Navy.

With my participation in the urban resistance, and the fact that my father had become a minister in a government that was openly opposed to the Germans, my brother and myself, then twenty-one and twenty-five respectively, had to go into hiding.

The German authorities were after us. A little later we attempted, along with my mother, wife, and our baby, Maria, to escape to the Middle East. We did not manage to get away, though we spent two nights hiding in a cave near the sea. Our house was requisitioned by the Germans and was ruined: we found very little of our belongings when we came back after the liberation of the country.

The last Germans left Athens on October 12, 1944. There was rejoicing and a spirit of elation and jubilance: it was a glorious day. A few days later the National Unity Government returned to Greece, and things appeared to be on the way to the establishment of a proper democracy.

But then something terrible happened. As if we hadn't suffered enough, two months after the liberation of the country, in early December 1944, civil war broke out. It was, on one hand, an all-out attempt of the Communists to acquire power by force and, on the other, an all-out attempt to crush the new popular movement. Both sides committed grave errors—not only errors but crimes.

The leaders of both sides wanted a confrontation. The people knew better and hoped for peace. The leaders of the Communist Party were generally narrow-minded Stalinists; their followers were generally broad-minded social democrats! On the other side, there were some idealist nationalists and many true democrats. But the keys were really in the hands of reactionaries. The civil war ended in early January 1945 only after the British had intervened to take an active military part on the side of the government. World War II was still going on in Europe.

Nicholas Plastiras, a man of known democratic and progressive tendencies, was called in to form a caretaker government that would pacify the country. Archbishop Damaskinos was named Regent. I think Plastiras was sincere and did all he could, but the Right, which had been victorious over the Communists, behaved disgracefully, especially in the rural areas, where a period of white terror followed. This was, I think, the basic reason for the third, and longest civil war (1946–1949), which broke out about a year and a half later.

Looking back on the tragic events of those years, the full history of which has not yet been objectively written, I think that E.A.M., both militarily and politically, controlled the real majority of the people upon the liberation of Greece. Nevertheless, it was finally defeated, in part through its own mistakes, and its followers underwent the painful experience of a merciless white terror. The cadres of E.A.M.–E.L.A.S. who are alive today generally agree that their leadership was mistaken, but they attribute their defeat primarily to the military intervention of the British in December 1944. British intervention was important, but it must not be forgotten that the *coup de grâce* was in fact given to the Greek Left by Stalin himself, who, through the Yalta Agreement, recognised the British right to control the fate of Greece.

This white terror was of unheard of ferociousness and extent, under the doubtful excuse that it was a spontaneous anti-Communist outbreak of vengeance, an unavoidable consequence of the previous red terror. Yet, even if we agree that there was some grain of truth in this argument, the rightist governments of the time should have followed legal, honourable, and constitutional methods to rectify injustice. Instead, state and judicial authority was tacitly handed over to irresponsible parastate rightist bands, basically composed of Security Battalion elements. These bands punished those who committed crimes during the occupation and during December 1944— and many innocent people as well. Within the rural population many victims of the white terror, and, to a certain extent, of the red terror, suffered reprisals of a personal nature that were in no way politically motivated. During this period, which was so charged with passions and hatred, courts-martial passed about 16,000 sentences, many of them sentences of death. When a revision was later permitted, about 13,000 of these sentences were annulled.

It was under the Minister of Foreign Affairs in the caretaker government of General Plastiras, the late John Sofianopoulos, that I first went to America, as secretary and interpreter. I was a young man of twenty-six. Sofianopoulos headed the Greek delegation to the San Francisco Conference (April–June 1945), which set up the United Nations. That was a very interesting experience for me. I saw America for the first time. I loved San Francisco, and the Americans in general impressed me very favourably. Their attitude then was a heartening one. They really believed in democracy, from government leaders on down. Being the Foreign Minister's aide, I saw a number of personalities of the time: I remember President Truman; Edward Stettinius, the American Foreign Secretary; Jan Christian Smuts, Prime Minister of South Africa; Anthony Eden, Foreign Secretary of Great Britain; Lord Halifax; Clement Atlee; Molotov; Georges Bidault of France; Paul-Henri Spaak of Belgium; and others. Alger Hiss was the Secretary-General of the American delegation.

In 1946 the first post-war elections were held in Greece. The Left and two small splinter parties from the Centre committed the serious political error—I myself remember agreeing with that line then—of abstaining from the vote because democratic freedom had not been fully established in the countryside. The Left commanded popular support, which would have given it about one-third of the seats in Parliament. If that had happened, the third civil war could have been averted, and we would probably have developed into a regular western-style democracy. But, unhappily, with the abstention of the Left, the great majority of the members of Parliament came from the Right. A rightist reactionary government was formed under Constantine Tsaldaris, and King George II returned to his throne after a plebiscite of doubtful veracity (not that he did not have a following, having become the symbol of anti-Communism). A little after that, the third civil war broke out.

On the one side, there was the Communist-dominated Left; on the other, at the beginning, there was the Right. As things developed, the greater part of the non-Communist forces of Greece took sides with the government of the Liberal and Populist parties—the Centre and the Right—under the old Venizelist leader, Themistocles Sophoulis. King George II died on April 1, 1947, and was succeeded on the throne by Paul I, his younger brother.

The third and longest civil war was another calamity for the country. It lasted until September 1949 and was finally won by the government. It was at that time that American intervention in Greece started, with aid given to the government in order to avert a Communist victory. This civil war can be seen from many angles. It can be argued that if it hadn't been for the war and American aid, Greece would be part of the Soviet block today. On the other hand, it was a victory of reaction, since it was the reactionary forces that really led the fight against the Communists. The extreme Right therefore acquired power, and the Greek Army was purged of any element that was in any way progressive. The way was paved for the troubles we have had since.

During the civil war the Makronissos (Long Island!) Concentration Camp was instituted on a barren island off the coast of Attica, where all citizens drafted into the Army who were not "nationally minded" (an expression of the time which included most liberal and progressive individuals except the actual Communists), underwent a period of physical and moral indoctrination. In fact, it was a concentration camp of the German type, and the prisoners were severely mistreated and tortured. The Commander of the Military Police under the dictatorship today, Colonel Ioannides, distinguished himself then (as well as now) as one of these torturers.

In 1950 fair elections were held. Five months after the end

of the civil war, the "progressive forces" (i.e., anything that didn't belong to the Right: Centre, Progressive-Centre, Socialist, and Communist) got something like 70 percent of the vote among them. Three centrist parties formed a coalition government, first under Plastiras and a little later under Sophocles Venizelos, the son of the great Venizelos. This coalition ruled the country for two years, until 1952. Unfortunately, they proved very weak, and there was much internal squabbling. During these two years, however, better living conditions prevailed, and the country started getting on its feet again after ten years of foreign and internal warfare.

In 1952, a general election was called again, and this time a strong rightist coalition named the Greek Rally, headed by Field Marshal Papagos, the former Commander-in-Chief of the Greek Army, won. Alexander Papagos, who proved in the end to be a very weak Prime Minister, ruled until his death in October 1955. Although that government had a very strong parliamentary majority, it also didn't live up to expectations.

When Papagos died, the era of Constantine Karamanlis began. He was one of the rightist members of Parliament and had distinguished himself as Minister of Public Works under Papagos, but his appointment as Premier didn't exactly satisfy constitutional law. He was directly appointed by the King at a moment when the Greek Rally, which still held the majority after Papagos's death, had called a caucus in order to elect a new leader. According to all indications, it would not have been Karamanlis. Nevertheless, Karamanlis ran the country through three elections, up to 1963. He certainly had a strong government that accomplished quite a number of good things, especially in public works, tourism, and monetary stability, but he strangely lacked the perspective to initiate truly popular measures in the fields of social work, education, labour reform, and the like. He and his party should be blamed, and blamed very severely, for carrying on the civil-war, anti-Communist, and anti-progressive witch-hunting atmosphere in order to remain in power. They felt that if the country really reached a purely peaceful period and persecution of progressives dubbed "Communists" stopped, they would very likely lose the majority. That in my view is the great wrong committed by the Right in post-war Greek developments: wanting to keep the civil war atmosphere hot for as long as they could, so that they could exploit it from an electoral point of view. During these years, the lack of a modern well-organised Socialist Democratic Party in Greece proved to be disastrous.

Another problem which must be at least briefly mentioned in this survey of post-war political developments in Greece is the Cyprus question. Cyprus is a large Greek island of 650,000 inhabitants, with a comparatively strong Turkish minority (19 percent of the population). As had been the whole of Greece, it was occupied by the Turks throughout four centuries. In the late nineteenth century, the Turks sold the island to the British, and it became a colony of the English Crown. After World War II, when most colonies were gradually being granted independence, the Cypriots, as was to be expected, asked for the union of their island with Greece. The British chose to resist this claim, and a strong guerrilla liberation movement was started by the Greek population as a result. Greece strongly urged Britain to grant the right of self-determination to the islanders, but the British Government took a completely negative stand and, what is worse, incited the Turkish Government (which as late as 1952 had stated that it was not interested in Cyprus and, in 1923, in the Treaty of Lausanne, had officially renounced any claim on the island) to support the Turkish minority and veto union of the island with Greece. Graeco-British relations got very strained; there were some anti-British demonstrations in Athens, but worst of all was the murder of Greeks and destruction of their property by Turkish mobs in Constantinople and Smyrna in 1955, under the complacent eyes of Britain and the United States. Finally, in 1959, a treaty was signed between the three powers and the Greek and Turkish Cypriots, which set up the independent Cyprus Republic. But trouble between the two communities actually never stopped, and twice (1964 and 1967) brought Greece and Turkey to the verge of war.

Throughout these years, from 1950 onward, I practised law in Athens. I found some satisfaction in it, but my heart was always in politics. I wrote political articles in the progressive newspaper *Eleftheria* (Liberty) and participated in the political life of the centrist-liberal parties. Twice, in the elections of 1958 and 1961, I was drafted, so to speak, by George Papandreou, with whom I had developed quite an intimate political relationship, to run for Parliament in the Athens area. In 1958 our party did so badly that only one member of Parliament was elected in Athens from the Centre. The experiment was repeated in 1961 without better results for me, although both times I got a good number of votes.

The elections of 1961 were rigged elections. The Right was beginning to feel that it was losing ground. Our party, the Centre Union, under the distinguished and able leadership of George Papandreou, who was already in his seventy-third year, actually waged a long and well-thought-out campaign denouncing the elections of 1961. It was carried on throughout 1962 and 1963, when the Karamanlis Government was in power, both in Parliament and at large.

During that period George Papandreou proved an excellent popular leader. He and the newspaper *Eleftheria*, with its distinguished editor Panos Kokkas,* played preeminent roles in

---

* Panos Kokkas, who was a friend from my university years, was an extremely bright and able man, and a decisive factor in the success of the democratic struggle of those years. George Papandreou confirmed this view in our last private meeting, about a year before his death, although he was no longer on speaking terms with Kokkas. It is a great

this struggle to maintain democratic institutions. The response of the people led us to our electoral triumphs of 1963 and 1964.* During that period I was active as Papandreou's representative and liaison with the youth movement of the Centre Union, which played a big role in the struggle. It was I who coined the famous democratic slogan of the 1960's: "1-1-4"† when I used it for the first time in a speech to the youth movement in a rally in Athens (April 1962).

The assassination of the leftist member of Parliament, Gregory Lambrakis, in May 1963, was the straw that broke the camel's back,‡ and the Karamanlis Government fell. I was on the threshold of active politics.

---

pity that *Eleftheria*'s editor, who admittedly had reasons to dislike the Papandreous, became blinded by political passion and sided with the apostates during the crisis of 1965.

* In a classic political blunder, which showed up the cynical position of the Americans, U. S. Ambassador Ellis Briggs chose to support the genuineness of the 1961 elections in his New Year 1962 message to the American colony in Athens.

† Article 114, Constitution of 1952: "The safeguarding of the present constitution is entrusted to the patriotism of the Greeks."

‡ This assassination is the subject of the motion picture *Z* by Costa-Gavras. Many people, after having seen it, have asked me how accurate the film was. I can say, with full knowledge, that it is as authentic as a documentary. I was one of the principle witnesses for the prosecution in the trial against the assassins of Lambrakis which took place in December 1966. It was clear to me then that his assassination was executed by extreme rightist elements in contact with the police and other government offices in Salonica, the second largest city of northern Greece.

6

IN ACTIVE POLITICS

In March 1963 George Papandreou invited me to his house and told me that he believed I should run for Parliament again. He thought I should be a candidate from Ioannina in Epirus, the part of the country where I was from. The local committee of the Centre Union in Ioannina had already asked him to name me as one of the candidates.

I had been thinking of this myself. I felt it was time I entered active politics as a full-time job. However, I was a bit cautious about deciding to run in Ioannina; although both my father and grandfather had been members of Parliament from Ioannina for a number of years, I myself hadn't actually lived there for long; I had spent most of my time in Athens. I thanked President Papandreou and said that I would think it over and make a visit to Ioannina. The warmth of my welcome there convinced me that it was my duty to run. The party had fallen pretty low in the previous elections. In the outgoing Parliament, there wasn't a single Centre Union member of Parliament from Ioannina; I was asked to rejuvenate the local party and restore its old prestige. Epirus had been a traditionally democratic area, which had gradually shifted to the Right in post-war politics. After two days' deliberation, I accepted the nomination.

Technically, the next elections were due to take place in the fall of 1966 (previous elections had been in 1961—a four-year term), but the atmosphere was such that elections might not be very far off. On April 5 I returned to Ioannina and delivered my first political speech in a rally held in a theatre. The theatre was packed, and there were many people outside who could hear my speech through the loudspeakers (which were twice taken down by the police and re-installed by my friends). It was a success. The atmosphere of Rightist intimidation against anyone from the Centre or Left was quite strong then in Epirus, and the rally had successfully broken the ice. It is not an easy thing to start a political campaign virtually from scratch. I wasn't well known; my father had been elected to Parliament in Ioannina for the last time in 1936, and my grandfather had died back in 1924. But as of that day I was baptised in active politics.

I came to love the people of Epirus, especially the people in the villages. The electoral area of Ioannina is composed of the so-called Ioannina prefecture. The capital, Ioannina, is a town of 50,000 inhabitants, and there are three minor towns of about 3,000 inhabitants each. The rest are villages—375 of them. The area is very mountainous and many of the villages are over 1,000 metres in altitude. They are very picturesque and some are quite old, with beautiful seventeenth- and eighteenth-century buildings. Except for a few major arteries, the roads are of dirt, and access to quite a number of villages can only be had on foot or by mule. Many of these rocky dirt roads are cut off by the rains and the snow in winter. So as of that summer, after buying a second-hand (I suppose twenty-second is nearer the truth) jeep of 1940 vintage, which had been all through Montgomery's campaign in North Africa, I diligently started visiting every village of my area. In many a village I arrived and met only two or three people. But from the very beginning there were villages where I received a warm welcome. Of course, I also met with some outright antagonism, if not hatred—but that's politics.

I soon found out that there were some villages that had been visited by candidates only once or twice for as long as the villagers could remember. I later came across two villages— Pyxaria in the Konitsa area and Vradeto in the Zagoria district—that had never been visited by a member of Parliament, not even by my father, who was a renowned walker and rider (there were no jeeps and no roads then). Before long, a strong grassroots organisation was going in my favour.

In May, the atmosphere of political crisis came to a culminating point. Gregory Lambrakis, member of Parliament co-operating with the Left party of E.D.A., was assassinated in Salonica. After the assassination of Lambrakis, the government weakened. The fall of Karamanlis came in June 1963 when he resigned, allegedly having fallen into disagreement with King Paul on a matter related to the latter's visit to London. (It has not been clearly proved whether that was an excuse for his resignation or the real reason.)

The King called upon Panayotis Pipinelis* (an extreme reactionary rightist figure of the Karamanlis party who was very close to the palace) to form a caretaker government composed of known extra-parliamentary rightist elements, which got a vote of confidence in Parliament. The new Prime Min-

* The man who became the Junta's Foreign Minister in late 1967. He died in 1971.

ister, posing as a neutral caretaker, announced that he would hold elections. Since the previous elections had been carried out under a rightist caretaker government completely under the influence of the palace and Army, our party considered elections under Pipinelis completely out of the question. On September 5, 1963, a huge and enthusiastic rally took place in Athens, at which George Papandreou spoke: he made it clear that if the King insisted on having the elections held, with Pipinelis as Premier, the Centre Union would not participate. That was a gamble which took political foresight and courage. The King was finally forced to give in. He asked Pipinelis for his resignation. Then, in the middle of September 1963, a caretaker government that was in fact neutral under President of the Supreme Court Justice Stylianos Mavromichalis, was formed, and elections were held November 3, in excellent order and with complete freedom.

Even though the elections were completely free, the atmosphere around them was not one to inspire confidence. The people had been so intimidated in previous elections that they were still afraid. To give an example (only one among thousands): about twenty days before the election, I visited the village of Derviziana in the Souli area of Epirus. I knew that there were some Centrists there. As usual, I had announced to the village the time and the day I would visit. I arrived there driving the jeep, with my secretary, Constantine Tatsis, a retired gendarmerie major of old 'democratic stock. The little square of the village was completely empty. I entered the café where village political meetings are usually held. There were two people playing backgammon in one corner of the room; they didn't even turn around. That they deliberately ignored me seemed odd. Even if they belonged to another party, the arrival of a stranger in a little village café always caused some curiosity. But they went on playing backgammon. The owner of the café greeted me and said, "Of course, you know, I belong to the E.R.E. (the rightist party), but I will be glad to give you a cup of coffee." And we sat there, all three talking away for a few minutes, not really having much to say. I asked about a few problems of the village. At the other end of the café was a group of about ten people. While I was talking with the two men at my table, they all stood up and walked out without looking at me, and in a moment, except for the two men playing backgammon, the café was completely empty. After a while, I said goodbye to the owner and took a stroll in the village street with Mr. Tatsis. No one came out to see me. We got in our jeep and went on our way. No more than half a mile from the village, round a corner of a narrow dirt road with trees and bushes on either side, two men jumped out and signalled for us to stop.

I whispered to my secretary, "What's this; are they going to beat us?"

"Could be," he answered, with his usual sangfroid.

We took it rather calmly. When we had stopped, the two men came over, took my hands in theirs, and said, "Oh, Mr. Mylonas, we were waiting for you. We wanted to see you, but you understand, it's not exactly the thing to do to meet you publicly. There might be people who would denounce us. Come with us."

We got out of the jeep and found a group of about six or seven other persons standing behind some trees. Then I recognized them; they were the people who had left the café! We talked of political affairs; they expressed their love of democracy and said how much they were against the rightist government that had oppressed them. Even with free elections, they felt such remnants of fear that they didn't wish to be seen speaking to me in the village. On the Monday after the elections I would be gone, but the gendarmes and the T.E.A. (National Security Battalions) would still be in the village. When the electoral returns came, I was very careful to notice how many votes we had received in that village: it was 85. Of course, the Right got a greater number, something like 300; but there were eighty-five people in that village on our side who did not dare come near me!

During the pre-electoral period, I had been very careful not to make any promises that I could not keep. I spoke of problems, of what we hoped to accomplish, and of my ardent devotion to democracy.*

The last week before the elections the two principle opponents, the Centre and the Right, held big rallies in a large square in Ioannina—one was on Thursday, the other on Friday. I was the speaker for the Centre Union and Mr. Evangelos Averoff, head of the E.R.E. ticket and former Foreign Minister, spoke for the Right. I spoke for about forty minutes. The speech was strong and enthusiastic, and it did a lot to bring about the final surge of votes to our party. I gave one big pre-electoral promise (after I had spoken about the matter with George Papandreou over the phone), worded very carefully. Should we win the election and form a government and found a new university, then Ioannina would be the site. The cheering this promise got was immense. It showed something which has always been characteristic of the Epirotes: their great love of knowledge, letters, thought, and science. Even in the small villages, this news not only gathered votes but

* The clientèle system, as the French call it, had through the 140-odd years of parliamentary rule in Greece often reached disquieting proportions. It had become a sort of habit for many a citizen, in the agrarian population mostly, to consider the candidate, and even more, the elected deputy, a sort of agent or commissioner for his personal problems. And the quality of those individual "services" often decided the political allegiance of the voter. This was basically a result of the great poverty of the rural population. Some of the more progressive elements among the Centre Union's deputies did quite a bit to change this atmosphere and carry political struggles away from personal favouritism and sterile anti-Communism to the support of principles and the projection of some elementary social pogram.

really created elation. That university was founded, and it has been one of the things I have done for my electoral area of which I'm really proud.

When the elections were held on November 3, 1963, our party emerged victorious, but not with a big majority; we got 42 percent of the vote nationwide; the Right got 39 percent; and the Left, 13 percent. One or two independent parties got a very small fraction. I was elected member of Parliament from Ioannina.

George Papandreou, as the leader of the party that had the majority, was called in by King Paul to form a government of the Centre which, however, did not command an absolute majority. The Left proposed to give us a vote of confidence, allowing the newly elected government to stay in power. But George Papandreou decided to call for a second election. He was confident that the people would give us the absolute majority. At the time I thought perhaps that was an intelligent move, but in the long run, I think it proved a mistake; it perpetuated the principle (which in fact violated the Constitution) that the Left must never participate in a government or even be part of the majority. The Right did not wish a new election and indirectly proposed to give us a vote of confidence instead. Papandreou was unequivocal and finally managed to have the Parliament dissolved only two months after the election. A new election was called for February 16, 1964.

With the new year, I settled in Ioannina again and started more campaigning throughout the area. (It was during the pre-electoral period that the associate leader of our party, Sophocles Venizelos, Vice-Premier and Foreign Minister in our first cabinet, died of a heart attack at the age of seventy-one while campaigning in Crete.)

The second election on February 16 ended in a real triumph for the Centre Union. This time we got 53 percent of the vote nationwide, and were able to form a government based on our own majority in Parliament; we had 171 members of Parliament out of a total of 300. I was once again elected member of Parliament from Ioannina. The elections were carried out by an interim caretaker government headed by Mr. Ioannis Paraskevopoulos, the Vice-Governor of the National Bank, a practise that has more or less become a habit in Greek political life, especially since the war.

This time I was not predestined to remain just a member of Parliament. I was made a member of the cabinet. I was at my mother's home, having just returned from Ioannina to tell all the news, when we heard over the radio an announcement from the Premier-Elect's office naming the new cabinet members who would be sworn in the next day. It was then that I heard for the first time that I was one of them: I was to be Secretary of State to the Prime Minister. While this job was really sort of head of the Prime Minister's office, it had gradually through the years acquired supervision over a number of state services. I was concerned with: Press and Information, Foreign Press, the Greek Archaeological Services, Greeks Abroad, Cinema, Sports, and a few other things.

During the first days I was in office, I called in the head of personnel, who gave me lists of the principal employees of the ministry and explained their work. I noticed a lot of overlapping. One man, George Georgalas, bore the title of "Soviet-ologist." I asked what that was about, and the head of the personnel shyly remarked that he did not exactly know; the man belonged to a semi-autonomous directorate. I also called in the Director-General of the ministry and asked him to report. He was rather cautious when he came to a service which was called "Directorate of National Enlightenment." He was evasive and said, "I think you'd better find out for yourself, Mr. Minister."

The whole affair sounded strange. The head of this directorate, a retired general, never reported to me, his new minister.

As a matter of fact, he had vanished. The post being vacant, I appointed George Bertsos, a brave and able journalist, to fill it. He was, for the people who have seen the film *Z*, the newspaperman who was so active in doing the job the police should have done in Salonica and who finally found out who the culprits in the Lambrakis affair were. When I appointed Bertsos, I told him to look into the directorate's doings very carefully and find out what it was all about. The Sovietologist Georgalas had been a Communist, and a leading one, allegedly having studied in the Moscow K.U.T.V. Institute. He had worked for a number of years as a speaker for the Greek language broadcasts of Radio Budapest, whence he used to launch oral bombshells against the "monarcho-fascist gang," as he called the governments of the Right in Greece during and after the civil war. Later he "sold his soul" to the Western secret services. He came to Greece and headed "psychological warfare" against "anti-national Communism." I fired Georgalas when I learned this.

Georgalas has since become a Junta minister. He has proved to be a regular fascist of the worst sort. The Georgalas case proves the falsification, or rather the counterfeiting process, which democratic forms of government have undergone in Greece, with the elevation side by side with the legal state of a gigantic illegal superstate. Later it was accidentally discovered that the Ministry of Defence issued a monthly magazine under the title *Sovietology*, printed in 100,000 copies and distributed exclusively within the armed forces. The editor of the magazine was George Georgalas. He collected a large sum of money monthly from the government, and this very government was being insulted repeatedly in the pages of the magazine! It became necessary for the Premier himself to intervene. He came across great resistance from the palace, the American Military Mission, and the army leadership before he was able to stop the publication of *Sovietology*. Needless to say,

Georgalas was also employed by the Armed Forces Radio Station. Twice I called the attention of the Defence Minister, Peter Garoufalias, to the matter, but to no avail.

Bertsos's investigation of the "Directorate of National Enlightenment" came up with some very interesting facts. One day he called on me to ask me to visit the directorate, which was located in premises of its own outside the principal ministry building. We went there together and had a locked chest of metal drawers opened. We found interesting things: one was "File No. 1193," which contained material on the organisation of counter-demonstrations against the Left and advice on ways to disseminate false information against the Left and the Centre. As Minister of Press, I released part of its contents. Finally, the whole thing went into the judicial file against the Lambrakis assassins. It showed the connection between the directorate and the assassination.

My period as Secretary of State to the Premier was interesting. I had a lot of different jobs to do. I was very open to the reporters and gave them any bit of news that I thought could be made public. About 99 percent of it could! There weren't any restrictions on the press, of course. The press had been free even during the previous rightist régime, but there was a law that forbade the printing of any special editions without authorisation from the Minister of Press. (The law had been passed at the time of the civil war in order to avert unrest, when special editions would appear throughout the day and their headlines would be shouted in the streets.) That was a law that should certainly be abolished, but this had to be done through Parliament, and it would take time. So I gave an order that all newspapers would be permitted to issue as many special editions as they chose, and in order to follow the proscriptions of the existing law until it was annulled, I presigned a number of such permissions and gave them to the editors of the Athenian dailies. They would just have to fill in the date and time of their special edition; and they could have special editions to their hearts' content. (As perhaps was to be expected, the number of special editions fell below previous figures!)

I took a number of other steps that showed that our government was a soundly democratic one. I had a number of conversations with the foreign correspondents accredited to Athens, gave a number of interviews, and tried to supply our press officers abroad with information. Several times I had to discharge employees who, until then, had merely been functioning as agents of the Right, not employees of the Greek government. I also worked a lot with the Greek Archaeological Services, which badly needed funds, and the Directorate of Sports. My relationship with my fellow cabinet ministers was generally cordial; and in some cases friendly. Working with Prime Minister George Papandreou, with whom I often cooperated on a number of matters, usually at his home and in the evening, was a real pleasure.

But I must admit that we lacked a carefully prepared program of government. The heads of the different Ministries, including myself, more or less did the best we could without really having a well-coordinated plan. We had the same general principles and line of thought, of course, which was important, but the lack of a detailed plan of action soon struck me. The Prime Minister issued instructions on how things should be run at the cabinet meetings every Friday, but that wasn't enough. I saw how much our party, and practically all Greek political parties, lacked a well-built internal structure—a characteristic of the Western democratic political parties—to make it ready to administer the country once it had won an election. This deficiency is something that we paid for.

Yet the government was very popular. It followed some sound policies, and I believe that our first year in office, if anything, increased our popularity. Most important was the atmosphere of complete democracy and liberty that our government brought to the country: this is something the people of Greece will always remember. They had gone through difficult days under the rightist governments, although there was nothing, of course, compared to the present hated dictatorship. But it was really a new atmosphere, a sort of New Deal that started when the government of the Centre Union came to power. A number of economic measures were taken (yearly per capita income increased), but I think that the best job was done in education. George Papandreou was Prime Minister and Minister of Education. The latter post was rather nominal, although he did give the general lines of our educational policy. He appointed a Secretary of State for Education, Loukis Akritas, who, together with the distinguished educator, the Secretary-General of the Ministry of Education, Evangelos Papanoutsos, brought about important educational reforms. How was I to know then that fourteen months later I would be asked by the Premier to carry on these reforms when Loukis Akritas, a man not more than fifty-four, would die following an operation? Papandreou asked me to change ministerial posts and to become Secretary of State for Education in April 1965. All of the following educational reforms were completed and added to under my ministry:

1. Free education. This was a basic step. Schooling at the primary, secondary, and university levels became completely gratis. The importance of this measure was especially felt at the universities to which many boys and girls did not venture because they lacked the funds. And we were only at the beginning: we had a long program that provided for free housing and free meals for university students.

2. Free distribution of school books.

3. Free school meals. These started in November 1964, and reached primary schools of all the Greek villages, though not the cities. There were many reasons in favour of such a

system. One of them was that children used to return home for lunch, many times two and three kilometres away, and would not always go back to continue their lessons in the afternoon. When the free school meals were inaugurated, the children would stay at school, where they had a good breakfast in the morning and a nourishing lunch at noon, and return home in the evening for their family dinner. These free meals were greatly appreciated by the rural population. They succeeded in bringing about an increase in attendance by 10–12 percent; they improved the health standard of the pupils (by 8 percent according to the October 1965 yearly medical exam); and they earned the gratitude of the parents by decreasing their expenses and enabling them to work in their fields throughout the day without having to worry about the children and their lunches.

4. Continued operation of the schools in the small villages. This measure has a special importance in Greece, where the exodus of the rural population toward the cities (and emigration abroad) reached alarming proportions after the war. The only way to keep the village alive—demographic data tell us that in a few years the opposite trend will start—is through modernisation: good roads, electricity, water, telephones, etc., and, of course, the upkeep of schools, although this might sometimes appear to be a disproportionate burden on the country's budget in the case of schools with very few children.

5. Increase of obligatory education from six to nine years, the minimum required by most European countries; some require even ten and twelve years (except, characteristically, Spain and Portugal).

6. A new, special method of teaching ancient Greek in the high schools. The difference between ancient and modern Greek is greater than that between Chaucer's English and modern English. Through the years, the nine weekly hours of ancient Greek had become very tedious and had virtually

ended up in a dry study of grammar and syntax. The Centre Union Government, wanting to stress the importance of classical culture, introduced, together with the study of the original texts, extensive study of ancient Greek literature in translation into the modern tongue. Thus, under the new system, instead of 10–15 pages a year from Thucydides or Euripides which were barely covered in high school, the students acquired full knowledge of the ancient Greek texts in translation and learned more of the teachings, the wisdom, the beauty, and love of freedom emanating from our ancient culture.

7. Another measure was the elevation in all grades of the demotic language (everyday spoken Greek) to equal status with the so-called pure language (an intermediate between ancient and modern Greek used in official documents, laws, scientific treatises, most speeches in court or in the Parliament, most newspapers, editorials, etc.).

8. Renovation and modernisation of history text books, in an effort to create a genuine national education, and not glorified, chauvinist, nationalist propaganda.

9. Civics in high schools. A lesson of democracy: the study of the Constitution and rights and duties of all citizens.

10. Introduction of "new mathematics."

11. Filling in vacancies of teaching personnel. In eighteen months 9,000 teachers (primary and secondary education) were appointed. And there still remained vacancies.

12. Introduction of the "academic diploma" (a new system of entrance into institutions of higher learning).

13. Creation of two new universities (Ioannina and Patras). Forbidding, by law, professors to teach in more than one university (the so-called flying professors, who spent their time between courses flying from one university to another).

15. New university buildings.

16. Increase in teaching personnel in all universities.

17. New equipment for the very rudimentary laboratories.

18. Founding of the Pedagogical Institute, the general staff, so to speak, of Greek education. This body was composed of top and enlightened educationalists and was of great help to the minister.

A number of other measures were initiated, the mention of which would make this report too long. But I will briefly state what happened to educational reforms under the Junta: school meals were abolished; more than 1,000 primary schools were closed; compulsory education was decreased from nine years to six; the new method of teaching ancient Greek was abolished, along with the equality of the demotic language; texts referring to democratic ideals were no longer made use of; history books were changed—all official histories contain a full-page picture of Papadopoulos, while Pericles occupies ⅛ of a page. Civics lessons were abolished; the "academic diploma" and the Pedagogical Institute were abolished; the elected boards of all student unions were abolished and Junta agents put in their place; hundreds of university professors were fired for their political ideas (many professors were appointed directly by the Minister of Education, not elected by the respective faculties); the rectors and senates of the universities became government appointees; military commissars were attached to each university; plainclothesmen infiltrated the student bodies. Today, the youth of Greece is taught the art of denouncing one's neighbour for his political ideas. And yet the huge majority of the students are anti-Junta!

What was the American attitude during our period in office? I sincerely believe that the American Embassy disapproved of our government from the very beginning. There were some members of the staff who more or less accepted us (it wasn't their job to accept us or not anyway), but even under Ambassador Labouisse, who was considered liberal-minded, one felt the United States preferred the Right and

The new Government takes over in Athens on February 19, 1964. Front row, left to right: D. Zakythinos, Minister to the Premier in the previous caretaker Government; Andreas Papandreou, Minister to the Premier; George Papandreou, Prime Minister; and George Mylonas, Secretary of State to the Premier. Photo Tsakirakis, Athens.

Minister of Education George Mylonas addressing Parliament in May 1965. Photo Floros, Athens.

A celebration of the twentieth anniversary of Athens's liberation from the Germans was held on the Acropolis in October 1964. Left to right, front row: Prime Minister George Papandreou (waving his hand); his private secretary John Manousakis; John Zigdis, Minister of Industry; and George Mylonas, then Secretary of State to the Premier. Photo Tsakirakis, Athens.

At the inaugural ceremony for the new university in Ioannina, the Prime Minister is greeted by a girl dressed in the characteristic costume of the Epirus region. Mylonas is on the Prime Minister's right. Photo Achilles, Ioannina.

Pepper trees shade the main square in Hora, where villagers gather to socialize and talk politics. Photo Eleni Kulukundis.

The village of Hora, isolated among the barren hills of the island. Photo Eleni Kulukundis.

One of the gendarmes, guarding the author from a "discreet" distance. Photo Eleni Kulukundis.

The house where the author lived, inscribed with the initials of the National Security Battalions, a paramilitary organization responsible for "combatting Communism." Photo Eleni Kulukundis.

The author, drawing water from the cistern in his house. Photo Eleni Kulukundis.

Mylonas reading on the terrace of his Amorgos house. Photo Eleni Kulukundis.

Mylonas on the terrace of his house in Amorgos. The escape plan was well under way when this picture was taken. Photo Eleni Kulukundis.

The rocky southern shore of Amorgos, not quite as steep as the area about two miles away where Mylonas made his escape. Photo Eleni Kulukundis.

the palace to our democratic and progressive administration. A characteristic incident occurred early in our tenure of office. We came to power in February 1964, and this happened in late April or early May. There was a dinner party at the Labouisses (Mrs. Labouisse is the daughter of the famous scientist Madame Curie). After dinner, the ladies went into the big salon and the men stayed in the smoking room, to talk business, smoke cigars, and exchange jokes, not always in good taste. (What an oriental and disagreeable custom, which, oddly enough, is not Greek but Western!) Those present on the Greek side were Admiral Toumbas, the Minister of Interior; John Zigdis, the Minister of Industry; Michael Papakonstandinou, the Secretary for Defence; and myself. On the American side were Labouisse and a few other diplomatic officers. At a certain point, Ambassador Labouisse addressed us, more or less along the following lines:

"Now tell me, my good friends, how did you manage to get that myth of fraud in the elections of 1961 through? It was a masterful way of doing it, really, because it caught the people's imagination; you had a good slogan to fight the government, and you finally got your elections much sooner than you expected."

And then we realised that the man obviously believed that the 1961 elections, which had been accepted by everyone as having been rigged (about 200 court rulings proved it), were genuine, and that our party had played a shrewd political game by denouncing the result of those elections. We couldn't believe our ears; we shifted the conversation from the jocular mood in which it had begun to a thoroughly serious one and said that we were really taken aback. We had never thought that the ambassador had such ideas; we gave him all sorts of instances of the fraud of the 1961 elections, which had been won by the Right, but I don't think we convinced him. It was then we realised how much the American Embassy had wanted a victory of the Right, regardless of the means, and how unhappy it was with our victory. And this happened before anything really wrong or mistaken according to the American point of view was committed by our government. That and many other incidents, especially those related to the members of the American Military Mission and the C.I.A. in Greece, show we were not liked, and go a long way toward explaining why, finally, the American administration is on the whole quite content to have a dictatorship in power.

The proud, independent stand taken by George Papandreou when visiting President Johnson in Washington to discuss the Cyprus question certainly increased American dislike of our government and probably hastened its downfall. The Prime Minister made it clear to the President that Greece was an ally of the United States, not a satellite. It has been rumoured that when Papandreou left, President Johnson told one of his aides, "One de Gaulle is enough on my hands."

During my term as Minister of Education, I was speaking in Parliament one day, explaining a law on one of the educational reforms that was being voted, when I was interrupted by a deputy of the Right who accused my Secretary-General, Mr. Papanoutsos, of being a Communist, which, of course, he was not. A sort of "McCarthy period" atmosphere still reigned in the rightist opposition. I answered, "Oh, why don't you forget these civil war slogans; they're outdated." There was a fury in the ranks of the Right in Parliament, and I think part of the Centre was also dissatisfied. How would I dare refer to a war that had officially been called the "bandit warfare" (the Communists were called bandits in the nationalist vocabulary of the time) as a "civil war"? But it was a civil war, and a war in which no foreign power had taken part. The Communists had, of course, gotten help over the border in materièl from the Soviet bloc, and the nationalists had gotten important aid from the United States, but not a single foreigner fought on either side. So I stood there insisting that it was a civil war; Greeks had been fighting Greeks whether we liked it or not. That was something that was held against me by the Right ever after.

The royal family in Greece had always been a centre of reaction. When our government came to power, King Paul was living through his last days, suffering from cancer. The Centre Union Government was sworn in on February 19, 1964, at the Royal Palace of Tatoi, thirty kilometres from Athens, in the presence of King Paul. It was the last time we saw him. Very pale, dressed in military uniform, he leaned against a piano all the time, which made it clear that he could not really stand up. He gave a short address, saying that he wished us good luck and that he would be at the disposition of the government. King Paul died in early March 1964 and his son, King Constantine II, who was then twenty-four, came to the throne. The fact that a young, new sovereign was taking office, a sportsman and an openhearted character, was considered a good omen. We would be able to start anew with the royal family, and the government of the Centre, which had basically been an anti-royalist party throughout its history, might find a good modus vivendi with the new King. As things turned out, perhaps it would have been better all round if King Paul had lived.

A few months after, the King married the young and beautiful Princess Anne-Marie of Denmark, and everything appeared to be in good order politically. But there were powers preventing the King from acting as a fully constitutional monarch, who would respect the government in power and play his limited role under the Constitution. These powers were led by the old royalist palace clique, a very reactionary lot. Two individuals who played an immediate role in influencing the King against the Centre government and George Papandreou were Queen Frederika, the Queen-Mother—a very ambitious

woman, still quite young, who poked her nose into everything—and the Secretary-General to the King, Costas Hoidas,
a judge who had, in fact, been my friend in youth and who, I
believe, played a role in the manipulations that eventually
brought about the government's fall.

The first crisis in the relations between our government and
the palace came when the so-called Aspida Conspiracy was
"discovered." This was an affair that, for all practical purposes, was staged, and it was a bit of nonsense at most. A
very few officers (about fifteen, in an Army that includes about
10,000 officers) allegedly created a sort of league to have
their interests protected by the government of the Centre, since
the great majority of army officers were against the government and openly rightists. The King, probably manipulated
by his advisors, looked on the formation of this league as a
great danger to the Constitution, interpreting it as a sort of
mutiny of the Papandreou Government (and the Papandreou
family) aimed at overthrowing him. Of course, nothing of the
sort was the truth. But it created a disagreeable atmosphere in
the relations between the Premier and the young King.

A politician who played an ugly role in this affair was Peter
Garoufalias, the Minister of Defence for our government. He
originally came from an old liberal and centrist family. But
when he married, rather late, into a very wealthy family, he
became a real reactionary, although loosely remaining in the
Centre Party (somewhat in the way that George Wallace
remains in the Democratic Party in the United States). Garoufalias was named Minister of Defence because George Papandreou wanted to have a conservative at the head of that
ministry to appease the officers who were unhappy to see the
electoral victory of our party. That was a great mistake, and
we paid for it dearly. Garoufalias very quickly proved to be
more of an organ of the palace and of the Right than a loyal
member of our party. And as relations began to deteriorate

between the Premier and the King, George Papandreou wanted to fire Garoufalias and take over the post of Minister of Defence personally.

Though it was none of his business constitutionally, the King vetoed this move, arguing that he would not accept Papandreou as Minister of Defence in view of the fact that his son, Andreas, was allegedly implicated in the Aspida Conspiracy. But if Constantine had confidence in Papandreou as his Premier, he could also have confidence in him as Minister of Defence. George Papandreou could have named any of his followers in Parliament as Minister of Defence and, again, the Ministry of Defence would have been under the Premier's influence. Therefore, I am sure that this was only an excuse on the part of the King.

By June 1965 it had become clear that the King was impatiently waiting to get rid of us before the next election. It was in early July 1965 that I first got a clear inkling that something was cooking. I had gone to one of the central auditoriums in Athens to address the annual meeting of primary schoolteachers in Greece in my capacity as Minister of Education. My speech about educational matters seemed to arouse very little interest. I spoke about a number of issues that had to do with the increase of the salaries of teachers, and still the interest was slight. Was I such a bad orator? But when, at a certain point in the speech, I remarked that it was uncertain how long we would remain in power, since that is the fate of a democratic government, there was a terrific outburst of clapping in the hall, accompanied by shouts of, "No, no, no; keep steady. Stay in your place; you should never move." I felt that the schoolteachers were perhaps more aware of what was coming than we were: that an out and out attempt was being made to get rid of us. As I finished my speech I said that it was probable the Premier himself would come and address the conference. There was a great ovation. I left the hall and immediately reported to the Premier's office to tell George Papandreou that I thought he should go and address those schoolteachers. He fully grasped the situation and said, "Let's go right away." We both entered the Prime Minister's car. On the way, I asked him, "What is wrong, Mr. President? I feel something is wrong," and it was then that he told me (it had not yet been announced to the cabinet and unhappily never would be) that he had received an insulting letter from the King that reminded him of "an *Acropolis* editorial" (*Acropolis* was an extreme-rightist newspaper).

I have never seen civil employees shout so enthusiastically as they did for George Papandreou when he appeared in the hall.

Days went by. July 15: in the morning, I presided over a meeting at the Holy Synod of Greece, the congress of Bishops (religion and cults come under the Minister of Education). We discussed routine matters of the church, and at a certain point I remarked, "I'm not sure how long I'll be in this position."

One of the Bishops answered, "We have heard the government is in difficulties. But you mustn't forget the great majority of the people are with you."

That same afternoon Parliament was in session. I was to speak for the government on one of the educational reforms. When I was called to speak, I noticed that the Chairman of Parliament, George Athanassiadis-Novas, was seated in his chair behind the tribune. That was about 6:30 on July 15, 1965. A discussion, a rather quiet one, took place on the educational bill. I was answering questions and explaining certain aspects of the bill when I suddenly heard a voice behind me, calling someone to order perhaps. I turned around and saw that the Vice-Chairman of Parliament, the late Emmanuel Baklatzis, was substituting for Athanassiadis-Novas. That often happens in Parliament, but usually the change takes place after the Chairman (or his substitute) has stayed in his seat for about three hours and become tired. The fact that Athanassiadis-Novas left after about twenty minutes is odd, in retrospect, although it did not strike me as such at the time: I suppose, I said to myself, that he has some other business and has asked the Vice-Chairman to carry on. But then, as I was speaking, one of the members of Parliament from the opposition, Mr. Costas Rallis, in a rather friendly, humourous way, interrupted me to say, "Mr. Minister, are you sure you are still in office?"

I answered jokingly that, for all I knew, yes, I had not yet submitted my resignation to him; but I also turned back and asked the Vice-Chairman if he thought there was anything wrong.

He spoke up and said, "Gentlemen, there is a rumour that the government has resigned. It might be false. I adjourn the session for five minutes until I find out."

And that was the end of our government!

As soon as the adjournment took place and the doors of the auditorium opened, the newsmen told us what had happened. George Papandreou, after having received two more rude letters from the King, had been to see him. He asked Constantine if he still insisted on not signing a decree whereby Garoufalias (the Minister of Defence who was undercutting the government) would be released of his duties and Papandreou himself appointed to that post. When the King again refused, Papandreou told him that he was planning to submit his resignation the next morning in writing (obviously in order to make a public record of his reasons). But the King said he would accept the government's resignation then and there. The King's haste appeared odd to Papandreou, who, however, left the palace immediately after. The audience had lasted four minutes. But what was even more odd was that half an hour later the Chairman of Parliament, a centrist, George Athanassiadis-Novas, was sworn in as Prime Minister (and Minister of Education). Stavros Kostopoulos, Minister of Foreign Affairs in the Papandreou Government, became Minister of Defence, and Admiral Toumbas, also a member of our party, became Minister of Interior and Public Order. The situation was peculiar; while the Prime Minister and the government resigned, someone from our own party had been called in to form the new government.

The reaction of the people the next day was heartening. Novas and his two ministers were ridiculed and called Apostates. Ever since, this title has stuck to the number of Centre Union deputies who gradually broke away to join these palace governments. There were street demonstrations in favour of George Papandreou, but nothing changed. After two or three days, more Apostates gradually broke away from our party. A parliamentary fight ensued, and it was a fierce one. Novas finally lost, 137–167.

When Athanassiadis-Novas submitted his resignation following this defeat in Parliament, there was still time, I think, for the King or his advisors to put an end to the political crisis that had been inflicted on the country: either by calling George Papandreou and giving him the mandate to form a new government, or by dissolving Parliament and asking the people to solve the crisis through their vote.

But the group that wanted to get rid of the Centre Union and all it stood for—progress, new social measures, and popular power—had plans to do away with the prospect of a really popular democratic government once and for all, even by force if necessary. Looking back, one can clearly see the fatal connection between July 15, 1965 and April 21, 1967.

A few days after Athanassiadis-Novas resigned, another figure of the Centre was called in by the King and given the mandate to form a government, Elias Tsirimokos. When Tsirimokos finally appeared before Parliament for a vote of confidence, those who stood fast were again victorious: his government fell; he got 135 votes against the necessary minimum of 151. Most people believed that by then the King had learned his lesson and that he would either call in George Papandreou to form another government or he would appoint an interim caretaker government to hold a new election: but he didn't do either. This time he gave the mandate to the other side of the Centre Union, to Mr. Stephanos Stephanopoulos, who had joined us in 1955 from the Right. Stephanopoulos just barely made it: 152–148. What went on those days was disgraceful. Members of Parliament were actually paid to join the Apostates. They would first be offered a ministerial post and then jump the fence: Stephanopoulos's feeble majority managed to keep him in power for fifteen months (September 1965 to December 1966).

Four days after our overthrow, George Papandreou, who lived in a suburb of Athens, announced that he would visit the Centre Union's central offices in the heart of the city. With that simple announcement, crowds amounting to probably a million people gathered along the way from his home to the offices of the party. It was then we realised that we commanded a huge majority and that the people were greatly opposed to the attitude of the palace; and that George Papandreou, once again, was a great popular leader.

But the King had not learned his lesson. The Stephanopoulos Government, supported by the Right, remained in power and, what is worse, behaved like a government of the Right. It was under that government that most of the Colonels who later carried out the coup were given key positions in the Army, and all sorts of anti-centrist, anti-democratic measures were taken. It was a disgraceful period in Greek politics. Why did the Apostates, who finally reached the number of forty-four, behave as they did? Were they so corrupt? After power? After money only? I think that all these propositions hold true for the rank and file. But their leaders? Was it only a great political mistake, or were personal interests involved? Such mistakes are crimes, and if there is one principal factor that precipitated the coming of the Junta, the Apostates were certainly the one. They dealt a deadly blow to democracy and parliamentary institutions.

With the fall of the Papandreou Government, a new period started in my political life. As of July 15, 1965, our party was in the opposition. I repeatedly spoke in Parliament on a number of issues, supporting the actions of the previous government usually in the educational field or in the different fields that had come under my jurisdiction when I was Secretary of State to the Premier; in this latter post, I had the possibility of using the so-called secret funds. There was an attack on our government for having increased the amount of this money. The Right claimed that the four ministers who had access to the secret funds (Foreign Affairs, Defence, Public Order, and Secretary of State to the Premier) had increased their use by 30 percent. I was proud to stand up and announce that the figure during my fourteen-month tenure of office amounted to zero. This question was an especially sensitive one because the previous E.R.E. governments had misused these funds a number of times.

George Papandreou did not report to Parliament during that period, to show his lack of respect for the puppet governments that had been installed and his disapproval of the King's manipulations. He would only go to Parliament when a vote of confidence was being taken. Instead, he turned to the people and made a number of political sorties throughout the country. I went with him on two of these, one in Crete and one in Thessaly. He was acclaimed by the people as a sort of messiah.

At the same time, I again visited the villages of Epirus. About twice every month I would spend five or six days in my electoral area, and gradually I revisited all the villages of the Ioannina prefecture. How much I came to really appreciate these people, usually simple people, up in the mountains or in the towns. They were amazingly well aware of the political issues at stake. They were also well informed about international politics. I will never forget the time I arrived in one little village, Ligopsa, late in the evening after having gone through four or five others. I sat in the café with the villagers assembled around me. First I spoke about the general political situation and the problems of the village. Toward the end of my conversation with these people—old people, young people, men and women—when the question period had come (I always invited questions, unlike most Greek politicians), an old man said, "Now, tell us, Uncle George [as they addressed me], a bit about de Gaulle; what is he up to?"

Greeks read newspapers a lot, and especially in these small villages they listen a lot to the radio, Greek and foreign. That's something that has kept the villages going in their anti-Junta attitude at this time. On one occasion I was visiting the village of Oxya high up in the Konitsa area, about 1,100 metres in altitude; it was winter and there was snow. My secretary, Michael Nikou, and I had left the jeep at the furthest point it could reach along the road, and we were mounting on foot, zigzagging up towards the village. A group of three villagers was coming down to meet us, holding lanterns. It was already dark by then and snow was very heavy on the little path we were taking. They reached us and said something like this:

"Welcome to our district; it's good of you to come."

I sensed a certain coolness in their tone. Because the path was very narrow and we were walking single file, Mr. Nikou, who was just ahead of me, and I could speak without being overheard. I whispered my apprehension to my secretary.

"Yes," he answered, "I have the same impression, and I can't understand what's wrong. After all, it was due to your endeavours that electricity was installed in this village. It was something they wanted so much."

"Are you quite sure it finally took place?" I replied.

"Yes, I am, but I wonder—after all, the Ministry of Industry finally okayed the installation of electricity in Oxya and we sent a telegram announcing it to the village."

"Oh, my God," I said, "what if it was never installed?"

We marched on up the mountain. From a previous visit, I remembered a point from which you could see the village clearly on a plateau to the right. The village was dark; there was no sign of light. I was ready to face the villagers' contempt for having sent them a false telegram. Before I had time to think much more, we had reached the first houses of Oxya, which were completely dark. It was about 8:00 on a cold December night when—and I'll never forget it—high up, obviously from the belfry of the church, I heard a voice shouting, "Mitso—now!" And then the whole village was lit automatically, and the church bells began ringing jubilantly. How moving it was to feel the gratitude of these people. The whole thing was so Greek: they had planned that little affair of pretending that they were displeased with me, of putting the lights out, in order to be able to give me the incredible surprise of seeing the joy of the village, all lit up and with the bells ringing! In the only tavern of the village, there was a wonderful meal prepared: roast lamb, cheese, milk, etc., and all the villagers were there, about one hundred inhabitants all told, I suppose. It was really an occasion! Politics has many bitter moments, especially when untruths go about and you have to fight them; when you see the ingratitude of certain people; when you have to fight with colleagues who don't exactly behave according to the best moral principles; but there are moments when one is really happy for the good one has managed to do. That evening in the little village of Oxya was certainly one of those moments. I went to bed at midnight feeling a whole village happy with me.

I now come to another subject. It was during this period that the star of Andreas Papandreou, the son of the Prime Minister, rose. As a minister of our government, he had not especially distinguished himself. I don't think he was accustomed to Greek politics, and he was not methodical by nature. But now, having taken a very intransigent position against our political foes and especially by bravely and openly and quite rightly condemning the palace and the Americans, he became highly popular. He said things and knew things we all felt, but perhaps no one before had formulated them so exactly in his epigrammatic way or presented them so well. So gradually he became a sort of hero of our party during the Apostate period, in a sense more so than our official leader George Papandreou.

But while taking the proper attitude, while in a sense going ahead of his times, Andreas Papandreou also managed simultaneously to commit errors, say the wrong things at the wrong time, and provoke unnecessary reaction by attacking everyone. He eventually became a controversial figure in our own party, too. I cannot really say whether his short passage through modern Greek politics has in the end been positive or negative. I will not, here, judge his activities after he was released from prison and went abroad, in January 1968. This is a completely different period about which I do not propose to speak at all in this book, if anything because I am also deeply involved in it. But in 1965–66, Andreas had become a symbol of the intransigent fight of the forces of democracy against the forces of the reaction.

In early December 1965, the trial of the assassins of Lambrakis took place in Salonica, and I was summoned as a witness for the prosecution. This is what the newspaper *Vima* wrote in part on the subject, under big, front-page headlines:

'I believe that the accused [gendarmerie] officers are the missing link between the actual perpetrators and the authors of the crime. They are blind executive organs of others. But this does not mean that they are exempt from penal responsibility. They must be morally insensible and unscrupulous individuals, and they bear full responsibility for their actions.'

This crushing statement was made yesterday before the Criminal Court of Salonica by the Centre Union member of Parliament and former minister, Mr. George Mylonas. With clarity and concrete facts, Mr. Mylonas denounced the para-state of the Right for the anti-democratic methods it used in order to neutralize whoever did not have friendly feelings toward the existing régime. The amazed audience heard Mr. Mylonas deposing in detail about the famous File No. 1193 and other documents which came to light during his ministry from which the relation between the iniquitous intentions that prevailed in top governmental echelons and the crime under consideration emerges manifestly. The witness stated further: 'There is a letter from Kostakos, in which the leader of the nationalist Elasites* mentions that he fought for E.R.E. and that he has dipped his hands in blood. And this letter is addressed to a public service! I ask you, why should a state service be interested in who worked for E.R.E.? And how does this individual dare to say he has dipped his hands in blood?'

The paper goes on to give the complete minutes of my deposition. Among other matters, I testified that the so-called Council of Studies of the Ministry to the Premier, under the Karamanlis régime, issued directives to the police and other parastate rightist organizations on how to foment anti-rallies during meetings of the Left and how to intimidate and even mistreat participants. Lambrakis was killed when such an anti-rally was staged in Salonica after he had given a speech in a closed hall. This council also issued instructions on how to spread false rumours against the Left. My deposition before the Salonica court lasted nine hours.

* A paper organisation set up by the Right during the period in question.

I was in Ioannina when, on December 20, 1966, the Stephanopoulos Government submitted its resignation. E.R.E. refused its confidence to this government and, not having a majority in Parliament anymore, it was obliged to resign. It has since been proved that secret talks had been taking place between the Right and Papandreou, with the King's knowledge, so that the stalemate in the political situation could be at last terminated. It was agreed that an interim government would be formed and an election called; should neither of the two parties acquire an absolute majority, the Centre Union and E.R.E. would form a coalition government. George Papandreou has often been attacked for reaching this agreement. Nevertheless, he assured return to constitutional and parliamentary order through elections, while he virtually conceded nothing. It was sure that our party would emerge victorious and that there would be no necessity for a coalition government with the Right, which was a very unpopular prospect at the time.

When Stephanopoulos fell, the King called upon Ioannis Paraskevopoulos to form a caretaker government, which surprised all of us unfavourably, because almost all its ministers belonged to the reactionary Right. It was then that Andreas Papandreou, correctly voicing public opinion at that moment, broke away from the party for ten days, saying that he would not on any account grant a vote of confidence to the Paraskevopoulos Government. From that point onward, the atmosphere became tense. While the rank and file of E.R.E. and the Left were heading in good faith toward elections, the military were busy mutinying to see what they could do to avoid one more Centre Union victory.

On March 4, 1967, my father, Alexander Mylonas, an oldtimer in politics, very nearly eighty-six and retired from public life for the past fifteen years, died a natural death at our home in Kiphissia. His funeral was a public one. And it was the last time that all the political parties were represented officially in a show of good will to an old political leader and parliamentarian. Everyone was there, from both Right and Left, and a big crowd attended. It was a moving occasion. I was glad that my father died and was buried under the democratic régime: he had just made it.

A little while after my father's death, the political situation came to a crisis. The reason—or the excuse—was that the famous Aspida Conspiracy was still in the air, and Andreas Papandreou was under a vague accusation for having participated in the plot. Being a member of Parliament, he had parliamentary immunity. The problem arose whether he could still enjoy that immunity under the Constitution during the forty-five-day period between the dissolution of Parliament and the holding of the next election.* There were rumours that the extreme Right was planning to have him arrested during that period. One legal view was that members of Parliament were covered by parliamentary immunity until the next election was held. Our party attempted to include in the electoral law that was being voted upon in those last days of the Parliament a clause specifically stating that members of Parliament are immune to arrest until the day the next Parliament convenes. This law was vetoed by the Paraskevopoulos Government, which shows how much that government played into the hands of the reactionary forces. Paraskevopoulos submitted his resignation. The King finally called in Panayotis Kanellopoulos to form an interim minority cabinet that was to hold elections on May 28. It was this government that was overthrown by the Colonels on the night of April 21, 1967.

---

* It's worth noting that the usually very slow-moving Greek judicial authorities issued a 100-page warrant against Andreas Papandreou, and had it typed and sent to the Public Prosecutor's office, who in turn sent it to the Minister of Justice; the Minister of Justice forwarded it to the Chairman of the Parliament—all in one day! This procedure would have taken at least three months in other cases.

7
CYCLADIC DAYS

I was on Amorgos in September 1968 when the notorious plebiscite took place in which the dictatorship had its new Constitution "voted" upon by the people. The result of this farce was 93 percent in favour of the new Constitution. When the day for the voting came, a Sunday, I was told by the Gendarmerie that throughout the day I should not go near the polling centre, which was located in the primary school house. What were they afraid of? That just my presence would influence the people?

The voting, as I heard from many of the friends I talked to in the usual clandestine way, was very simple. The voting committee was composed of people completely unknown to the villagers who came from afar. An infantry lieutenant was present. The villagers were presented with one ballot only, with Yes printed on it, and they were shown the urn and asked to throw the ballot in after putting it in an envelope. There was supposed to be a ballot saying No, too, but there was no question of choice; nor was there the possibility of going behind a curtain for secrecy. Thus, every single man and woman in the village voted Yes—what else could they do under the eyes of the military man?—and the result was 181–1. Everyone wondered who had managed to find a ballot with No printed on it in the first place, and who had dared cast it anyway. Whenever I asked anyone, he would candidly reply that there was no way of knowing. I suppose it was decided to report one No vote just to make the voting appear more plausible. The results were similar all over the country, and the Colonels had their Constitution "voted" under martial law. Ever since they have been administering the country dictatorially, without even applying that Constitution.

Many stories circulated to illustrate what a mockery this plebiscite was. Out of hundreds, I remember one that got much publicity in the international press. An American family of tourists, seeing all cars bearing bumper stickers or windshield signs with Yes (obligatorily put up by all citizens) decided to put a No placard on the back window of their car. The police were immediately mobilised. The car, which bore American plates, was hunted by two police cars for a whole hour through the streets of Athens. Finally it ended up in a garden-driveway of the U.S. Embassy. The American family left the car and entered the building. The police followed them inside. Only after it was officially proved, in the presence of an embassy officer, that these daring agitators, father, mother, son, and daughter, were American were they left alone, but with the strictest recommendation to take down the No sign from their car. So much for the freedom of a totalitarian plebiscite.

One day, when I was looking at a map of the Aegean Sea in the grocer's shop, I realised that I could associate practically every island with some exile. When I went home, I jotted down their names on a piece of paper, which I still have. The island of Tilos, J. Papaspirou and Karambellas; the island of Nisyros, Manavis—a deputy from Salonica and a good friend of mine; on the island of Leros, a camp with about 1,000 detainees, mostly rank and file of the Left and a few of the Centre; the island of Anafi, Hassapidis—member of Parliament from Macedonia and also a friend; Kithyra, Philip Mavros; Kassos, George Rallis; Aghios Efstratios, Angelousis, Alevras, and Vassilatos; the island of Yaros, a big concentration camp with about 1,500 more; Crete, a camp of about 300; Skopelos, George Mavros; Mitylini, D. Papaspirou; Folegandros, George Kavounidis; Kithnos, Brigadier Hörshelmann; in Kimolos, Generals Peridis and Vidalis; Thira, Colonel Papaterpos; Naxos, Admiral Spanidis—it was an endless list. Then, looking at the Greek mainland: Mikis Theodorakis in the mountainous village of Zatouna in the Peloponnesus; other fellow detainees of the Maroussi jail in central Greece. And last but most important, those in the innumerable jails in the country, the real martyrs: Filias, Iordanidis, Panagoulis, Notaras, Zannas, Filinis, Veryvakis, Lendakis, Plaskovitis, Kyrkos, Sophoulis, Nestor, Protopappas, Mangakis, Angelidis, Karagiorgas, Deloukas, Politis, Sipitanos, Dedes, Maltsidis, Pyrzas, Loukas, Kombotiatis, Kotsakis, Konstandopoulos, Tsagarestos, Filias junior, Michalakeas, Koniaris, J. Papadopoulos, Papamargaris, Vassiliou, Papazisis, Kapagerof, Pakos, etc., etc., etc. What a situation! And to think that practically all these people had been arrested with no specific accusation or with accusations that would be dismissed by any court in a democratic country, just because the dictatorship was afraid they might act against it.

It must be a very ugly feeling to be a dictator: to know that the people hate you, to pretend that you think they love you, to speak of democracy when you know that it doesn't exist, to speak of a free press when there is censorship, to say people are not tortured when they are. I wonder what a dictator thinks of when he is alone. The Greek dictatorship is a unique one in the sense that it has no following whatsoever. There have been dictatorships such as Hitler's or Mussolini's or Franco's that had some sort of popular following, if not the majority of the people behind them. In this case, though, it was just a small gang of army officers who seized power, or, as has been so aptly remarked, who highjacked Greece one spring night. They were not "brave officers." Not one of the Colonels has bragged of any distinction on the battlefield though Greece was involved in God knows how many wars during their lifetime. Nearly all of them were officers who made a career in the secret services and became very adept at making secret plans, which they finally carried out for their own benefit. A number of them collaborated with the Nazis during the German Occupation.

One of the matters I had left pending when I was arrested was the question of my son, Alexander's, leaving for the United States. Having just graduated from Athens College, he had received a scholarship to go to a university in Florida, and I was very eager that he get to America on time. When I was arrested on August 14 he had not yet been granted a passport, although his academic year started on September 1. I was afraid that things would get worse following my arrest. So they did. Letters from my wife vaguely hinted at what was going on. The boy was sent from office to office, reprimanded, so to speak, about his father, and intimidated. By September 1 he was still in Athens. He reported to a number of police officials and finally appeared before General Velianitis, who was then the chief of the special security forces. He was given a lesson on how to behave abroad and told that his father and Melina Mercouri were not good Greeks, among other things. My son had been properly schooled by his mother to answer nothing so that he might be able to leave; we were primarily interested in his following his studies outside the country, out of reach of the dictatorship. Finally, on the morning of September 12, he was granted the passport. My wife and daughter took him to the airport. Only after he had actually flown out did they inform me that he was safely out of the country. That was a relief to me. My second daughter, Eleni, lived in the United States; she had been recently married to Elias Kulukundis, a Greek from America, a writer, a bright and good man about whom more will be said further on. He and my daughter played an important role in the organisation of my escape.

My wife was permitted to come to see me for a few days, three times while I was there. She stayed with me in my house. I heard news from Athens, rumours, whispers, accounts of how things were getting along, family news. After her last visit in the late spring of 1969, I asked her not to come again in view of the fact that I was preparing my escape. I didn't want her to appear connected with it in any way: she might suffer for it. My brother also visited me twice.

The first of November 1968 brought news of the death of George Papandreou. He was the leader of our party, and he had reached his eightieth year—a grand old man. Perhaps he had his weak points, as any human being does, but he had been a very able leader, especially in the last years of his life. I don't think I have ever met a man with greater personal charm. I was deeply moved when the news of his death reached me over the radio. He had a very short illness of three days and died in the hospital. He rendered one last service to the Greek people after his death: his funeral became a huge gathering and rally for anti-dictatorship Greeks. It was said that the figure probably reached 500,000 people, chanting slogans against the dictatorship, shouting, "No, no, no"—the vote that allegedly got only 6 percent in the plebiscite! It was a tremendous show of force by the democrats in Greece, but I think it paved the way for the stricter measures of the dictatorship that followed. In a sense, perhaps, it happened at an inopportune moment, because it put the dictatorship thoroughly on guard. The dictators became sure that the people hated them and didn't want them. I don't believe Athens had seen such a rally for years, perhaps only on the liberation of Athens from the Germans in 1944, or when George Papandreou had been forced to resign in 1965 and had passed through the capital in his car on July 19. When he died there was a deep feeling that a whole period of Greek history had ended, to be succeeded by the grey days of the rigid, ignorant, and oppressive dictatorship of Papadopoulos. Who would have thought at the time that in 1973, four and a half years later, the dictatorship would still be in power!

While it was never made quite clear whether I was permitted to have a radio or not, I had brought with me a little shortwave transistor that wasn't taken away from me. I put it in a cupboard so as not to attract attention (the policemen came to my house once in a while) and always tuned in at low pitch. Having a radio was important to me. Every evening I would tune into the Greek language transmission of the B.B.C. and, what was perhaps more interesting, the German radio, the so-called *Deutsche Welle* in Greek, which gave a lot of news about the dictatorship that one couldn't learn otherwise. I also had the patience to listen to Athens radio, to find out what the dictators had to say. It was often tedious, but one must always study the doings and sayings of one's opponent. At noon, I would listen to Paris radio, the O.R.T.F., in Greek, a very good broadcast. All these Greek voices from abroad—Nikolaou, Andriopoulos, Terrenzio, Stylianou, Miss Evi, Maropoulos, Mavridis, Soteriadis, etc.—became my close friends, and the friends of thousands of other Greeks. They were there every day, giving hope, information, joking sometimes. They rendered us a great service, for which we all felt grateful. I hope they will be remembered when the country is liberated one day.

Hearing these broadcasts took some of my time, and it was

very helpful. My brother used to send me the Athens news-papers. Since they were censored, there was not much in them; but one felt life going on through those papers, with reports of friends who got married or died and other news items of every-day life. The local press from Ioannina was also sent to me. From time to time my brother also slipped in a copy of *Le Monde*, when there was something interesting about Greece. The censorship of the parcel of papers sent by post wasn't carried out very meticulously. As a matter of fact, my wife once took the great risk of slipping a note withing the pages of the papers. It was in place when I received the package.

As I have said, when one of the shopkeepers wanted to tell me something, he would have recourse to the simple device of calling out to me as I was going by to say he had gotten some-thing in stock that I had asked for earlier. But there were people in Hora who didn't have such a simple way of getting in touch with me, for instance the dear old midwife or the old couple mentioned earlier. So we found another device. When, for example, the midwife or the local priest wanted me for some-thing, they would throw a stone on the little veranda outside my door on the upper floor of my house. Whenever I heard the pebble fall, I would know someone wanted me. One pebble corresponded to X, two pebbles to Y, three to Z (five was the biggest number) and the throwing was usually done by small children in the respective families. It had been previously arranged how, where, and roughly when we would then meet. The pebbles were thrown on my little veranda from the tops of other houses, not from the street because that might be seen by the police. Many a time while I was sitting on a cold winter day reading, wearing my overcoat, of course, a pebble would fall. I would wait to see if there was a second or a third so that I could learn who wanted me. Sometimes extremely useful pieces of information were transmitted to me this way. I wish I could say more!

Repression came to the island of Amorgos on the third or

fourth day of the dictatorship, when "preventive terrorism," a classic totalitarian practice, was applied. The head of the police from Thira came over and called in about ten men and one woman, one by one. The woman, as could be expected, was the midwife. The men he just very quickly and without saying much hit and hit hard. After the beating he said, "This is to teach you that now things have changed and you should keep quiet."

The rather natural question that came to my lips when I heard this story, and had it checked from a number of sources, was, "Well, what did you do? Didn't you react?"

"Oh, no, you don't hit back at the police! Then you can really get into trouble."

The woman was not beaten, but she was thoroughly insulted with dirty words. She remained calm and answered nothing. (This doesn't mean that other women have not been beaten and tortured, when arrested for anti-government activities). One man was actually deported from the island and exiled to another island so that he would be away from his own centre of activities.

There was a rather easy, indirect way of finding out who these ten people were. They were among the first to make friends with me, and many times they indirectly sent messages. But there was another test, too: when you have been a member of the cabinet in Greece, you are customarily addressed by the title "Mr. Minister," regardless of whether you are in office or not. So most of the villagers, when they met me in the street or when I entered their shops, greeted me with, "Good morning, Mr. Minister; good night, Mr. Minister." Shortly after I arrived in Hora, an order was issued that if it were necessary to address me, I should be addressed simply by my name and not by title. Most people continued to address me in private as "Mr. Minister," but there were some who insisted on doing it rather openly, and they could be overheard by the policeman following me. Among these people were all ten of those who had been beaten, which shows how force brings exactly the opposite results.

Despite these contacts, loneliness settled in. The winter days were endless. It got dark about 5:00. I read and read and read, but that got tiresome in the end. The house did not have electricity, and I spent about two months with a petrol lamp. Happily, a little later, two technicians who were travelling through the different villages installing electricity came by; electricity made a great difference, and played a part in the method whereby I finally succeeded in escaping.

My house was on top of a small mound, and I could see practically the entire village clearly. High up, to the left of my house, was a hill on which there had been windmills in the old days. They were all out of use by now, except one, where a guard was usually stationed to watch my house, my terrace, and my movements. That was something I wasn't aware of at first. Once I found out I took appropriate precautions.

It was cold in Amorgos, much colder than I would have thought for a southern Aegean island. The village was located at the top of a mountain, 600 metres above sea level. There was almost always a very strong wind blowing on the unprotected village. So when winter came, it became quite cold. I spent the first three months without taking off my overcoat at all during the day in the house, and wearing two pullovers. I sat and read with a blanket over me, and I used to pull my hand out from underneath the blanket just to turn a page. At about Christmas time, my wife brought me a stove that made matters a little better, but even then the room was far from being well-heated. I could see my breath as one does outside in winter. My sleep was generally good, and except for the times when arthritis made my shoulders ache, I really rested in Amorgos. Parhaps I should be grateful to the dictatorship.

The town of Amorgos had once been much more densely populated but now it was a very small village. Gradually people had moved to the cities. It still had some quite large houses, many of them empty. Amorgos boasted of the first high school in modern Greece. The gymnasium, as we call it in Greek, was a building dating from 1829 (the Greek nation was liberated from the Turkish yoke in 1827), and the people of Amorgos were proud to say that they had the first gymnasium in free Greece. (I have a feeling it was the third one, but anyway. . . .) The island has, as do most areas in Greece, a very long history. Some of the cycladic marble statues found in Amorgos are renowned and are exhibited in the Athens Archaeological Museum. Simonidis the Elder, one of the most important poets of ancient Greece, came from Amorgos. I wasn't able to see it, but near the port of Katapola, there's an old Acropolis, full of ancient ruins—walls and buildings and what may have been a theatre; but it has not been taken care of by the archaeological services for years. There's a fifth-century B.C. wall not very far from the village. The island also has certain Byzantine and medieval remains. All these things were an interesting diversion for me, especially since I have a strong inclination towards history and archaeology.

As the days went by, I began hearing over the radio that my friends who had not been exiled while I was in Maroussi were being sent to different places. And I repeatedly heard of the arrest and torture of friends as these events became known outside Greece. I heard of the trial of Vassilis Filias, my good friend in Democratic Defence, and of his eloquent plea before the court-martial. In the summer of 1969, a big batch of arrests of Democratic Defence cadres took place. Some of those arrested were men I had directly or indirectly asked to join Democratic Defence. Despite my concern, I was the last person who could help them now. And then stories of their being tortured started coming in. They bore it splendidly, and impressed the world in their great trial before the Athens Court-Martial in March 1970. They were sentenced to heavy prison terms ranging from three years to life.

In the little place I lived in, events that are unimportant in cities take on a great magnitude. One day in September, all the church bells started ringing as if something very important had happened: the Bishop of Thira had come to visit the village. He was given quite a welcome; women went down into the street and kissed his hands. The next day being a Sunday, he officiated at the church, and I attended the service. I was impressed once again with the fact that the average Greek is not basically religious, but usually goes to church to celebrate some festivity or an occasion related to a national rather than a religious event—there are exceptions, of course. As it happened, while the services were being held I suddenly didn't feel well and I nearly fainted. I was taken out. There was a lot of hushed talk in church. I don't know what was really wrong with me.

There was a fisherman in the village who used to leave with his son at about 2:00 A.M., weather permitting, to descend all the way to the sea, get into his little boat, and fish. He would usually return at about 11:00, and when he arrived in the village, he would blow into a big shell that sounded like a ship's horn. The first time I heard it, I didn't know what it was. Later it became a pleasant signal of everyday life. Around noon, when the weather was good, I would always hear the fisherman's bugle, and the women from all the houses would stream out to buy fish.

About an hour's walk from the village was a small church older even than the monastery, the church of St. George Valsamitis. An inscription dates it from 787 A.D. Near the church is a little fountain which, in the old days, was considered miraculous for healing wounds, for telling the future, and so on. Once a year, Methodios, the abbot of the monastery, went to this church to hold religious services. My archaeological interests were aroused, and I asked if I could go. I was granted permission. A gendarme, Hercules, came with me. We took a very early morning walk to the ancient shrine and were just in time for the services, the gendarme and myself being the only members of the congregation.

It was a happy occasion in the fall when the whole village went out to the olive groves for a week to gather olives. On my walks, I could hear them singing, joyfully hailing me, and I would watch them bringing down the olives on large sheets strewn under the trees. These they would pick up and take to the communal mini-factory that produced olive oil, usually just enough for the villagers' own use.

There were a number of local customs in the village. Every year on December 18 the nameday of St. Modestos was celebrated. He is considered to be the patron saint of the animals. So one day every year the animals were given special treatment: dogs and cats were well fed, and horses, mules, and donkeys were not used at all. They lay in the fields all day and were given extra food and stroked by the children.

Once I was invited to a house. It was Christmas, my wife had come, and the local priest, Markos Despotidis, invited us to come and have dinner with him.

"Are you sure you don't mind?" I asked.

"No," he said, "I have only God to answer to." So we went to his house.

He and his wife had a very pleasant dinner for us. We spent that night in a family atmosphere, with the warmth of people around us. The next day there was trouble. The priest was called in to the police and interrogated for about three hours. "What were you talking about?" he was asked. Other people were asked if I was the only person invited and whether they had seen anyone else going into the house. The whole thing happened because we had gone out for a short walk and did not return home but went directly to the priest's house. The gendarmes lost trace of us for some time, until someone reported that he had seen us entering the priest's house. A mountain out of a molehill! I don't suppose that one conversation with a village priest could overthrow a government, but, there again, where's logic in dictatorships?

I was originally exiled to Amorgos for six months. The six months ended on February 14, 1969. As that date drew nearer, I wondered if my exile period would be extended. I had a notion of what was coming, because a few days before the exile sentence of the Brigadier had been extended for another three months. February 10 I got my extension order, too, the usual order of the Ministers of Public Order and Justice, saying that I was "still dangerous to public order and should therefore continue to dwell in the village of Hora on the island of Amorgos for another three months." That brought me to May 14, 1969. Well, as May 14 approached, I again began to wonder what would happen. The Brigadier had in the meanwhile been transferred to another place. On May 3 I heard over the foreign radio that my exile period had been extended for another six months. So I knew of it before I was actually handed the order and even before the sergeant knew! I was given the order on May 12; it extended my exile period to November 14, 1969. I was not predestined to be there for the occasion.

A friend sent a telegram to let me know I was going to receive a package with food. The package arrived; the driver of the car brought it up and left it at the grocer's shop. The police told the grocer that he could give it to me, and I picked it up. Then, a few days later, I received a letter from this friend mentioning that she had sent me the food and asking if I had received it along with a telegram. I had received the parcel all right. As a matter of fact, I had eaten practically everything in it by the time I read the letter; but I had never received the telegram! So I asked the men at the post office about it. They were taken aback.

"Oh, yes," answered the telecommunications man, "it came. But I didn't think it was worth telling you because I knew from the driver that you had already collected your parcel!" I found out later that the man had actually asked the police whether he should give me the telegram right away since I had received the parcel anyway. The sergeant coldly answered, "Don't ask questions and give him the telegram in four days' time." I mention this episode to show the degree of nonsense dictatorial régimes can reach.

While I was in Amorgos, the chief of the Gendarmerie at Thira came to inspect the island twice. Both times I was called in for a conversation. The first time, the chief, Captain Theophanidis, an ardent rightist and devotee of the régime, tried to lecture me on the good points of a dictatorship. I, of course, responded with my democratic beliefs, and that was the end of our meeting. I learned some time after that he had been fired for having embezzled some money. The second officer, who came about six months later, just asked me if I was all right, and if I needed anything.

The government had set up a group of National Security Battalions (T.E.A.) in Amorgos, as it had in all parts of Greece, as a parastate organisation "to fight Communism." Allegedly, all civilians from the ages of twenty to forty would have to serve, regardless of their regular military service.* In our village, only four men were called up, and these were never changed because the dictatorship had no confidence

---

* T.E.A. had been set up during the civil war in the zones that came into direct contact with the guerrillas, but never in the islands. It is a shame that this institution had only been restricted, but never actually abolished, by the Centre Government. The Junta, of course, revitalized it all over Greece, eighteen years after the last guerrilla had disappeared.

in any of the other people! These four armed men used to patrol the village all through the night, two by two, the first two until midnight, the second two afterwards. During winter, when it got very cold, they mutinied and said they could not carry on anymore. The police couldn't do anything about it and just accepted their protest, calling them back in service only in April.

On April 21, the date the dictatorship had been proclaimed, an official announcement was posted saying that the headmaster would address the village on the meaning of the National Revolution; the presence of all villagers was compulsory. Although the threat was obvious, when the time came for the schoolteacher to speak there were only five villagers in the square. I remember being amused to watch all the gendarmes going about the houses, knocking at doors, going into the two cafés, and ordering people out into the street and into the square to hear the speech. And yet, I don't think more than thirty people finally assembled to hear the oration. The schoolteacher who gave the speech did not believe in the dictatorship. He was acting under orders. As a matter of fact, the text of his speech was sent to him from Athens.

Members of the faculties of the primary and high schools had to deliver public speeches about the good things the dictatorship had done for the country. There was a young physics teacher whom I encountered at the tavern occasionally. We would smile at each other, and I quickly understood that she was on our side. One day, through the auspices of the shopkeepers, I got a message from her. She wrote, "Please help me. I have been ordered to address the public next Sunday on the economic policy of the dictatorship. What can I say? I don't know anything about it." So there was I, an ardent enemy of the dictatorship, trying to defend its policies. I answered back, advising her to mention a few generalities. Then I got another message saying that she had received a list of items she might discuss. I told her that the best technique was just to connect all these items together in a rather incoherent way that would not make much sense. I added, "Anyway, our Prime Minister's speeches don't make any sense either." Later, when I met the girl in the street, she was smiling broadly. She whispered that she had given the speech on Sunday and it had come off all right, in the presence of about ten people! She's long gone from Amorgos now.

I would like to mention another matter because it bears on my attitude toward the dictatorship. An obviously well-meaning relative had tried to get me released on grounds of health, because of the heart attack I had suffered. But she did it without informing me. I will never forget how mad I got when I found out. We had quite a little family row through letters that didn't go through the censorship. It infuriated me because I was forced into the position of asking a government I despised to take pity on me. The point is not that I bore my hardships "heroically," but that our determination not to have anything to do with the gangsters who were running our country was absolute.

Listening to the speeches of Dictator Papadopoulos on the radio, one comes to understand what a folly a dictatorship is. I have never heard anyone before so thoroughly abuse the Greek language, and, of course, he thinks he is an eloquent orator. He makes repeated mistakes, always trying to speak in the most old-fashioned, so-called refined Greek, which he tries to use without knowing how, so that he never really ends a sentence. You can never understand what he is talking about. I always listened to his speeches with interest; they were a good reminder of the tragic conditions of our country.

On January 3, 1969, I was called to the post office early in the morning to be told that there was a commotion at the Gendarmerie because a message had come through that I would be receiving a call from the United States at 3:00 that afternoon. They couldn't forbid it because they wanted to make sure that the United States believed ours was a free country. I found out later, through the usual channels, that the operator was told to make doubly sure that the line with the police station was connected as soon as I started speaking; that the Naxos gendarmerie major would also tune in to hear what I was saying; and, finally, that a major-general at Piraeus would also be listening to my historic conversation with the United States of America. At 3:00 the call came in. It was my son and daughter who were in America. It was a very short conversation. They said they just wanted to hear my voice and wish me a happy New Year. I was moved to hear theirs. We exchanged a few family words and that was all. What a tempest in a teapot!

It was while I was in Amorgos that Alexander Panagoulis (the man who made an attempt on the life of the dictator in the summer of 1968) tried to escape from prison. I could not decide whether this was a real escape or just a fake one, staged by the dictatorship in order to arrest more people and bring about a feeling that the régime was omnipotent. The news came out that he had managed to escape and then, three days later, he was arrested in a flat in Athens and taken back to jail. I thought that the feeling of helplessness that came over the people when he was rearrested was really what the dictatorship was aiming at. He was in a military jail with officers and men all around him; it would have been quite difficult for him to get out, and it could well have been a staged affair, the informer being in on the secret from the very beginning.* I was one of those people who felt the sorrow of his being rearrested, after having been elated by the fact that he had managed to escape.

And thus, day in, day out, time passed. . . .

* I have since been told by Stathis Panagoulis, the prisoner's brother, who lives in Italy, that it was a genuine escape, which was given away to the police by an informer who collected the price set on Panagoulis's head.

8
PREPARING THE ESCAPE

About two months after I had been dispatched to Amorgos I started thinking that my life there was of no help to the resistance of the Greek people against the dictatorship, and that I should try, if possible, to escape to Western Europe, where a political movement against the Junta was developing. While I was in Athens, I was engaged in resistance work although called in to the police repeatedly, and at the time I believed that escaping abroad was not the right thing to do. Now, secluded on the island, I became useless. Of course, just the fact that I had been arrested was a service to the cause. My name was on the lips of many people as an opponent of the dictatorship, and the fact that I was going through the ordeal of exile worked against the Junta. But that wasn't enough, and I began to think seriously of the possibility of escape.

My first findings were negative: I was in a mountain village, at least an hour's walking distance from the sea, very well supervised, with my movements checked all the time. It seemed impossible. However, I started carefully and diligently working on this idea of escape, noting details which at first glance would seem to have no special meaning, and yet which proved to be important—details of everyday life, of the movements of my guards, of life in the village. Gradually, the escape plan began taking vague shape in my mind.

It was impossible for me to escape during the night; my house was closely guarded by two armed guards, and there was also a detachment of T.E.A. patrolling the village all through the night. My house had only one exit: even if I managed to get out through a window, which was not at all easy, I could very well encounter one of these patrols and be arrested. So the escape would have to be during the daytime. I signed the book at the Gendarmerie twice a day: at 9:00 A.M. and 6:00 P.M. Between 9:00 A.M. and 6:00 P.M. there are nine hours, but between 6:00 P.M. and 9:00 A.M. there are fifteen hours. Obviously it would be better to escape during the fifteen-hour period than the nine-hour period. That would give me more time to get away. So I gradually formed the opinion that the best time to escape, if there was to be an escape, was immediately after signing in at 6:00 P.M. If I managed to get away unseen, in theory I wouldn't be looked for until next morning at 9:00 when I wouldn't show up to sign the book. Of course, that was simplifying matters. Where could I go, and wouldn't they be aware of my absence?

But then the plan gradually took shape. If I left after 6:00, it would have to be in summer when it was still daylight, to give my guards the impression that I was still around. I would have to use the moment when I was able to get out of sight during my walks. So I more or less decided on the time. It would be a little after 6:00 in the evening, and in summer.

If I did not return from my walk, obviously there would be

a lot of uneasiness and a search would take place. Even if I managed to reach the coast at some solitary place and board a boat, the alarm would be given, and the boat would be caught before it could get very far. So the first test I made was to see how much my absences were noticed and how my guards would react. It was still winter, when I would take my morning walk between 11:00 and 12:00.

One day I told a friend, "Look here, I want you to tell me exactly what happens while I'm away on my walk today."

I don't know what he thought I was talking about. He just said, "To be sure, I'll let you know."

Perhaps he had already begun to suspect that I was planning to escape, but we never exchanged a word about it. I took a newspaper in my hand and walked out of the village, followed as usual by the guard on duty. He stopped a little way outside the village and sat on a rock, while I continued out of his sight, walking steadily. I deliberately didn't go far that day. As soon as I got out of the policeman's sight, I went and sat behind a rock, which I had already picked out on a previous walk (it was very near the village, not more than 150 metres away), and pretended to read my paper. But I purposely did not return on time, that is, within twenty minutes or so. I looked at my watch. Soon it was half an hour I had been away and then forty minutes. Nothing happened. When I had stayed away three-quarters of an hour, I got up and started back. The moment I emerged from behind the rock, I saw two policemen walking rather quickly in my direction. They immediately slowed their pace, and, as I reached them, said hello in a rather nonchalant way. I returned to my house.

The reason I hadn't gone very far is obvious; if they had actually reached me, they would have seen me very near the village absentmindedly reading a paper under the cover of a rock in the winter sun. They would most likely have said, "Oh, there you are," showing that they were pleasantly surprised that I hadn't gone far, and that I had just forgotten myself while reading.

The next day, my friend informed me: "Here's exactly what happened yesterday. The guard sat for a little while and then began looking intently toward the path you had taken. He looked at his watch two or three times, got up and walked up and down a little, and then, instead of following you, he came back into the village and went to headquarters. A few minutes later he returned with another policeman. They started walking quickly in the direction you had left by. And it was then that I saw you returning."

So that was the first test. It was quite clear that I wouldn't have enough time to move away. They would be after me very quickly, and they had their antennae up for anything out of the usual.

After that, I decided on another stratagem, one that would induce my guards to think I had returned to my house unseen and was safely in my room, while (if the plan worked out) I would in fact already be far away. I started taking very irregular walks in order to condition the policemen to the regularity of my irregularity, so to speak. When something happens every day, for days on end, it can appear regular and become accepted. There were very many paths out of the village. One day I left for a walk in one direction. Five minutes later, I came back. Another day, I left in the same direction, passed behind some rocks, and returned to the village in fifteen minutes from another direction while the gendarme was still waiting for me at the other entrance to the village. He got a bit uneasy, came back, and asked a villager if he had seen me.

"Certainly, Mylonas is up at the central square," would be the answer.

I wasn't doing anything illegal from their point of view, and they didn't make any remarks about it. The next day, I would start from another exit and return the same way. The third day, I would go out from yet another exit and return from the first. I was careful to repeat my stunts for every guard who was on duty. It was never the same sequence of guards: for example, Manolis on Monday, Hercules on Tuesday, Aristeidis on Wednesday, and so on. I was never able to predict who would be on duty on a given day. That was rather a misfortune, because some of the policemen were less vigilant than others. Gradually I got them conditioned to the fact that I didn't have a prescribed program of walks; every day I did something a bit different, and the time it took me varied. I even confessed this, so to speak, one day when I went to sign the book in the presence of the sergeant and two other policemen.

"I'm getting sick and tired of these walks," I said. "By now I know every stone around the village, and in order to create a little diversion I try every day to take a different sort of walk." They took that in and accepted it; I even saw faint smiles cross their faces, as if to say, "Ha, ha, we know; we've noticed it." But that was exactly what I was after: their noticing it.

After three or four months of this game they were conditioned. The time came for me to go into the second phase of my tests. I asked another friend, one whose house was strategically located near mine, to tell me if the guards noticed when I put on the light in my house. That proved easier than I thought. The next day, and again on other occasions, he told me, "Yes, the moment you put on the light in your house, the guard on duty sort of puts his head up with satisfaction, very clearly showing, 'Ah, he's there: he's back.' " By now, as the summer came on, my walks took place after 6:00. I would return, go into the house, and put on the light. So I had the guards conditioned to my taking very irregular walks, from the point of view of both duration and itinerary, and to accepting the fact that I was back by seeing the light go on in my house. That was very important: if things went as usual, a good portion of my plan of escape would work.

The time and the way of escape had therefore been more or less determined: after 6:00, during my walk one day, I would not come back. But something else had to happen, too: the light in my house had to go on while I was out, even though I was out of the house. I wouldn't be missed until the next morning at 9:00 when I didn't show up to sign at the Gendarmerie. The night guards would be watching an empty house.

I started thinking of getting an accomplice. My house was not guarded while I was away, or at least I remained under the impression that it was not; it was me they were after, not the house. I didn't see why someone couldn't get into the house, put on the light at an agreed time, turn it off at 10:30, spend the night in the house, wait for the time when the night guards would leave (there was always a period when the house wasn't strictly guarded, between about 7:00 and 8:00 A.M.), and get out of the house unseen. Then, at 9:00, I wouldn't be there. But that wasn't an easy proposition; I couldn't really ask someone else to run such a risk for me. I was sure there were many islanders who would have been ready to do it, but, I thought, the fewer people in the plan, the better.

I then considered another device: I checked how much oil was needed for the oil lamp to burn for about four hours, from about 6:30 or 7:00 in the evening until 10:00 at night. I would light it before leaving. It would not be seen from outside with the sun shining. When dusk came, the house would have a light on. No one would notice the exact moment it was lit, and the guard would think I had lit it at a moment when he wasn't looking. Then, by 10:00 or 10:30, the oil would be used up, and the lamp would go out by itself. It would look as though I had put it out to go to sleep.

Then the question came up of having electricity installed in the house. I thought it was certainly worth it from many points of view. Since the escape plan was still very undecided and tentative, I went ahead and had electricity installed. The electricity in Amorgos, as I have said, doesn't stay on all day. It starts at about 3:00 in the afternoon and goes until midnight. It comes back early in the morning, and continues until 11:00 or 12:00. That gave me another way to solve my problem. I would put on the light while it was still daytime. The light would probably remain unseen since I lived on the second floor of the house. At midnight, the light would go off automatically, and that would be the end of that. If it went on again in the morning, no one would see it because by then the sun would be up. So I decided to start going to bed late. Midnight in Amorgos was certainly very late. Many times I actually went to sleep with the light on; it would go off by itself at midnight.

But I had to abandon this plan, too. On Easter, 1969, light was provided for my village and the little port for twenty-four hours a day. As a matter of fact, the machinery for it had already been available, but an extra employee was needed for a third shift; when he was finally appointed by the local commune, there was light throughout the twenty-four hours.

So that ruined that plan. I would have to do something different. I sat and thought, and then figured out that I could send to Athens for one of those automatic timing devices that turn electricity on and off at given times. They were very popular with housewives, who used them to regulate stoves while they were away at work. If I was able to acquire such a device, I would fix it in such a way that the light would go on automatically at 6:00 or 7:00 P.M. and off at 10:30.

Well, I put that in my little computer. What was my computer? An old copybook I had hid in the basement of my house, behind a lot of rubbish. Of course, the policemen could have found it if they had made a very thorough search, but why should they? So into that copybook, which I ironically named the computer, I used to feed all sorts of information and ideas. The problem was, of course, how I could get hold of the mechanism.

What else did I feed into that computer? Well, for one thing, I made all sorts of notes about what the guards used to do. For instance, one of the questions I asked myself was: should I escape on a feast day or on a regular day? Should I escape on a day when the ship from Piraeus came to port or on another day? Well, the computer—i.e., repeated observations I gradually accumulated—gave me the answer. Feast days should be avoided as much as possible: instead of being less strict with me, the guards had a tendency to become more vigilant. They seemed afraid that, because of the general relaxation during Christmas or Easter or other festivities, I might pick just such a time to escape. Security measures tightened up on me on days like Easter Sunday. Then there was the question of the ship. Its arrival, usually every week, was always a sort of social event. But the sergeant and one or two gendarmes would go down to see who got in and out of the ship. They would be away for a number of hours. The guards who remained in the village became more vigilant instead of less so because their chief was away. They felt the responsibility for me and the other exile was entirely theirs. That also ruled out a day when the ship came to port. As I will explain, I did not escape from the side of the island where the port is, but from the opposite southern side, which descends very abruptly to the sea.

I had not yet contacted anyone about my escape because there was another important matter to be seen to first. Where would I go to? I bought a map of Amorgos, which the school children used. It was a big, detailed map. I noticed that the southern shores were completely uninhabited, and descended very steeply to the sea. Hora was something like 600 metres above sea level, but I had no way of knowing what the land-scape down to the sea was like because I couldn't go far on my walks. I waited for a very rainy day to walk further away and find out a little more about my locale. It was spring or late winter. I didn't have long to wait before a very rainy day came along. Fortunately, the rain stopped at about 11:00 but the clouds remained, and it looked as if it would soon resume.

I started on my walk and a little after I had left, a big shower came down. Everybody hid, even the mules and goats. I used this occasion to make a dash toward the place where I had calculated I could start the abrupt descent to the sea, the hill overlooking a little bay where a small ship might come in and pick me up during the night. I took three pills of Trinitine, the medicine that makes my blood vessels widen in case of stress or danger, thus reducing the chance of a heart attack. Remembering my old days as a sprinter, I ran along until I reached the top of the place from where I planned to descend toward the sea, and, as it was still raining and no one was in sight, I even started going down for a few yards. I saw that the descent was difficult—it was very steep—but I thought that with some care I could make it. I came back drenched, but I probably gave the impression that the rain had overtaken my usual walk before I could find a proper place to take cover.

Now I knew where I would go. But still I had to do a little more checking. For that I used yet another friend. He, like a number of other villagers, went fishing from time to time. One day I asked him in a casual way how he managed to reach the southern shore of the island to fish. In two or three sessions (we avoided talking at length even though the police couldn't see us) he told me how. If he was beginning to guess why I was asking these questions he didn't show it. He just pretended to be describing how he went down with his friends to fish. He said that there was a certain tree (I had noticed it) from where they started. There was a path that could not be seen very well which brought them to an old unused manger. From there on, the descent really became difficult; they traveled down the bed of a rivulet located about fifty metres to the left of the manger. In the summer it was dry. This path made all sorts of odd turns and curves and jumps, but in the end it took them down to the sea. The plan appeared possible—not very safe, but feasible. The time had come for me to contact the outside world.

My wife had come to visit and I had already vaguely confided my plans to her. But then, in early June, my second daughter, Eleni, who was newly married, got permission to come and see me with her husband, Elias. I explained my plan to them at length. They were enthusiastic about it. What I mainly wanted them to do was to find and send me a device to put the light on and off automatically and to locate a caique, or small boat with a motor and proper crew, to come at a given time in the early evening, pick me up, and take me away. I told them where I thought I should go, since I had made a careful study of the map. I explained a rather simple way of locating the little bay on my map of the area; it wouldn't have been wise for them to take a map of Amorgos with them when they left. The cooperation of my daughter and son-in-law was invaluable, and I think it is safe to say that without them the escape would have been impossible.

They left a little while afterward. Since they were going off to live in the United States, it was rather easy for them to find an excuse to return to Amorgos a month later—to say good-bye to their father for good. When they returned in July they arranged to send me (I cannot mention how at this time) the automatic electricity device and a mechanism whose use I didn't understand immediately. It turned out to be a walkie-talkie, or rather one part of a walkie-talkie; the other part would be on the boat that would come pick me up; they also sent me a big flashlight. Then the important question of the boat came up. It was proving difficult for them to find the proper people to board a yacht or a caique and come and pick me up. Elias mentioned a few trips he had taken, none of which was satisfactory. He promised that I needn't have any doubts: in the end a ship and a crew would be found on time. We had agreed in principle that the crew would be composed of tourist-like foreigners, including women.

Then, consulting my notebook, I told them that I thought the right time from many points of view—moon, wind, sunset, etc.—would be September 11. We agreed after some discussion of the pros and cons that on that day, without any further notice, I would make all the necessary preparations and leave for my walk never to return; I would reach the little bay and be picked up at about 7:30 or 8:00 in the evening.

Then a question came up. What if they could not come on the eleventh? So we went into a long consultation figuring out ways of contacting each other. We agreed that my daughter would telephone me. In the last analysis the telephone was the safest way of communicating: she was a member of the family; it was natural that she call me. But, of course, we prepared a code. We said that if, for some reason or other, September 11 was no good, my daughter would just make general conversation during the call, saying nothing very special, asking me about my health, etc. Then it would mean that I would be met on September 15. If, while she was talking, she mentioned a fruit, then it would mean another date. We set up a list of thirty-one fruits. I kept a copy hidden where I put my "computer" and she put her copy in her bra. It was rather difficult to find thirty-one fruits—we certainly used "dates" as one of them. If the date she mentioned by code was before the eleventh, it would mean that it was the corresponding date of the next month, October. If it was to be after October 10, we agreed on another code. But we considered any attempt to escape after early October improbable, because the seas tend to get rougher and, most important, there aren't many summer tourists left travelling about in yachts. The boat coming to liberate me would draw too much attention and might not even reach the island without trouble. In summer and on into the early autumn, the seas of Greece are full of tourists with their yachts.

My children were about to leave when Eleni said, "Suppose, finally, they cannot come upon this third date either."

"That's easy," I answered, "there would be another call mentioning another fruit, although too much of that wouldn't be too good."

Eleni didn't like that. After thinking a little I came up with a solution: "I think," I said, "we'll do something much more daring, but there is no other way." The people on the yacht would come to the island officially on the northern side where the port is. They would disembark, come up to the village as regular tourists, go out to the monastery and visit it, and then, when they returned from the monastery, go have lunch at Mrs. Aspasia's tavern at the time I had my meal: 1:00. They would not, of course, speak to me, but there would be some signal of recognition. When I saw them, I would know that the plan was on for that very night. They would then go down to the port at 3:00, leave, take to the open seas, and later, when it got dark, go around the island to the southern coast at about 8:00 P.M. to pick me up. That is how I would know the date: the day I saw them at lunchtime at Aspasia's tavern.

We all thought that possibility was not a likely one, but we agreed on it, and as it turned out it was a good thing. We thought it would be wise to have the signal of recognition something quite obvious. Among the books I had received from home was one I had not yet read entitled *The Tragedy of*

Lyndon Johnson. It had a big red and black cover so I could see it clearly. I gave the book to my daughter and son-in-law, and they took it with them. Was it predestined to return to Amorgos, I wondered.

There was one final detail we agreed upon. If, despite the above arangements, my rescuers were not able to be at their rendezvous on the fixed night, I would wait for them until dawn. I would not be able to return to the village at night anyway because I would immediately be caught. If the whole night went by without their being able to reach the little bay, they would then come back the next night at the same time. If that couldn't be done, the operation would be called off, and I would be informed of another date through the telephone-fruit system. Last, and most difficult of all, after spending the whole night hidden near the sea, I would try when the sun rose to return to the village and get into my house at about 8:00 A.M. This was the most difficult and daring part. First, no one must see me climbing up that impossible cliff. Second, could I, anyway, succeed in climbing that near precipice after a sleepless night and in my health condition? Third, how would it look if I was seen entering the village in the early morning? I would try to give the impression that I had just taken a morning stroll a little after the time the night guards had left. All that wasn't easy, but I thought the risk was worth taking.

With that arranged, we took leave of each other, purposely letting the policeman overhear that Elias and Eleni were leaving for the United States and that I wouldn't be seeing them for a long time. Then I was alone again. Waiting.

August passed. September arrived. I had known before setting the date for escape that on the evening of September 11 the sun set at 6:42 and the moon came up at about 1:00. When I was boarding the ship everything would be dark.

As the day drew nearer, I was ready, and somehow certain

that the whole thing would be a success. I have always been an optimist, and it has served me well in my life. In the early morning of September 9 I was informed that I would have a telephone conversation with Athens at 11:30 that day. I didn't like that message. Telephone calls were very rare, and since it was very near the prearranged date of my departure, the call might well be Eleni giving the news that things were not going according to plan. At 11:30 I reported to the post office. It was Eleni all right. She was sort of jolly and casual, and I said to myself, "Oh, here she is telling me that it will be the fifteenth of September," but as she was finishing the conversation, she said: "You know, you should always drink a lot of orange juice and have pressed oranges because it's good for you. They have vitamins."

Of course, everything we had said had been heard by the police but we had said nothing suspicious. As I left the telephone booth and was returning home, I kept saying to myself, "Oranges, oranges, oranges," to be sure I did not forget the proper fruit. After we had gone to the trouble of listing all sorts of odd fruits, it had turned out to be "orange," a daily household word in Greece. Well, I got home, went down to the basement, found my computer, and looked up "orange," and orange corresponded to the nineteenth of September. That meant a postponement of ten days. That made me think (and the supposition proved correct) that my rescuers were in trouble; if the postponement had been only a few days, it would mean that the boat was within Greek waters. For my rescuers to ask for a ten-day postponement meant that they hadn't yet left the country they were coming from on their way to Greece. By the way, we had agreed that the yacht would certainly not leave Cyprus or Italy or Lebanon or Turkey or France and come directly to Amorgos, because that would appear suspicious. The rescuers would make a tour of some of the best-known islands such as Hydra, Mykonos, Corfu, or

Rhodes and finally, sort of casually, be in Amorgos waters on the agreed-upon night.

I didn't have anything else to do but wait for the nineteenth of the month. Things were beginning to look worse from certain points of view: for one thing, the sun set at 6:20 on September 19, which was pretty near the time I would sign in and start on my walk; and starting out on a walk when dusk was approaching might appear a bit suspicious. Anyway, it had to be the nineteenth: I couldn't do anything else. The tenth went by. On the eleventh, I decided to make a test as if I were actually leaving that day, to see how matters would have worked out. The day went by smoothly. It was 3:00 P.M. when something took place that happened very rarely, not more than three or four times while I was in Hora.

I heard a knock at my door. I opened it, and there was Manolis, one of the policemen.

"The chief would like a favour from you," he said.

"A favour from me?" I asked.

"His boss from Naxos has come to Amorgos and will soon arrive in our village. It is probable that he will ask to see you."

I had been called in twice before in this way in similar cases.

"The sergeant would like to ask you, therefore, not to go out on your little walk. That way, if his chief asks to see you, he can produce you in no time."

"Oh," I said, "I'll do that with great pleasure. Why not be helpful?"

Manolis left. What a coincidence! I wouldn't have been permitted to go out on a walk on the very day I was planning to escape. What would I have done? I think I would have gone anyway, taking all sorts of precautions. I couldn't miss that rendezvous with the yacht! It would not have been easy at all. I would have tried it, but it would probably have failed. I stayed at home throughout the afternoon and the evening of the eleventh, and, as it happened, I was never asked or called for by the major, who left next morning.

Well, the eleventh went by, the twelfth, the thirteenth, the fourteenth, the fifteenth, the sixteenth of September. It was on the very morning of the nineteenth, when I was quite ready for the execution of the plan, that I was again asked to report to the telephone. It was Eleni again. She was a very good actress.

"Oh, daddy," she said, "we're leaving for America now. I thought I'd call you one final time to say goodbye. Have a good winter."

For a moment I said to myself, "The whole thing is off and that's what she's telling me." But she went on.

"I will be sending you that book you asked me for so you can continue your work."

I must say, it was the only time I sort of lost my sangfroid for a moment.

"Yes, my dear girl," I said, "send it, because I have run out of material at exactly that historical period." I was allegedly working on a history book and I could not continue my work for lack of a proper bibliography. "When will it be?"

"Oh," she said, "I can't be too sure, but I suppose within the next week or so. As soon as I get it from abroad, I will post it to you."

"Goodbye, be good. . . ."

That was the end of that.

So the nineteenth was not predestined to be the date of my departure. The problem now mostly came from the fact that the sun was setting earlier and earlier as days went by. The twentieth passed, the twenty-first of September—nothing. The twenty-second of September—nothing. On the twenty-third, at about 11:00 A.M., I was sitting on the little veranda outside my room, reading, when I thought I saw tourists. I immediately walked down onto the 21st of April Avenue. Tourists they were, sure enough, because the guard had come to stand near me, as he always did when foreigners came to the island. There was a group of about nine or ten people on mules and donkeys, crossing the village, obviously going to the Byzantine monastery. The first two were ladies, rather aged, in their sixties I'd say, and very clearly British. Those following were younger people, talking in English among themselves. I wondered if this was the group that would pick me up, after having been carefully selected in a way to make it appear as nonsuspicious as possible. Perhaps one of the old ladies was Alec Guinness in disguise! As the cavalcade came near me, I looked all these people very earnestly in the face and examined the things they were carrying to see if the book was there. But they just looked at me the way they looked at the wall behind me. I didn't impress them in any way! I thought perhaps they were playing their game very well, because I knew that my rescuers would have been shown a photograph of me.

Time seemed endless. At 1:00 I went to have my lunch, but the tavern was empty. There were no tourists to be seen. I wondered what had happened. Were they my people or were they not? September 23 was rather late in the season for tourists to come by. I addressed Mrs. Aspasia loudly in the presence of the policeman.

"I thought I saw some tourists this morning. Didn't they come by to have their lunch here so that you could make a little money?"

"Oh, no," she said, "just a little while ago they went by on their way to Katapola—they're leaving."

That ended my expectations, although I was left with a little doubt lest by any chance there had been a mistake about the place of the rendezvous. That day went by, too.

The twenty-fourth of September, nothing. The twenty-fifth of September had nearly passed when, late in the evening, having tuned in on Athens radio at the time of the weather bulletin (I used to do it three times a day during those crucial days), I heard that the seas were extremely rough, that heavy winds were blowing in the southern Aegean—exactly in the area where I was—and that all small craft had been prohibited from sailing. Well, I said to myself, they're not coming while this is on. On the twenty-sixth, the weather got a little better and by the evening the weather bulletin spoke of calmer seas; ships were being allowed to go out of port. On the twenty-seventh of September, with the sun beginning to set earlier and earlier and the situation getting rather difficult, something happened that I didn't like at all. I had tuned in to Paris radio at 1:15 for the Greek broadcast. It gave the general news and didn't have anything very specific to say about Greece. But then, toward the end of the bulletin, there was an alarming item.

"The *New York Times* has published an article about the conditions of exile and views against the dictatorship of the former Greek minister and member of Parliament, George Mylonas."

"Oh my God," I said to myself, "that doesn't come at a very opportune moment!"

What had happened was that I had smuggled out the article about three months before, to be published in a paper abroad. It had gotten into the *New York Times* at this very inopportune time. That wouldn't go unpunished! My co-exile, Mikis Theodorakis, who was in the village of Zatouna in the central Peloponnesus, had to suffer after having smuggled out one of his songs and an interview. He wasn't permitted to leave his house at all for quite a while. What if something similar happened to me? I might be summoned to headquarters at Thira to be interrogated on how I had contacted the reporter. And I would miss my rendezvous with the boat! What an unlucky coincidence.

Of course, one could look at it from another side, too. If a man is preparing to escape, he doesn't give interviews attacking the dictatorship; he poses as a good boy and avoids such things. Anyway, there was nothing I could do about it. I just kept my fingers crossed. By the time the Greek Consulate in New York had translated the article and sent it to the Security in Athens, and orders had been issued against me in Amorgos, I might well have left. That afternoon, as I was walking through the village, my friend the exiled airman expressed uneasiness when he saw me. He whispered as he went by. "Did you hear the Paris broadcast?"

I said I had. We walked a little way up and down and we met again; that was the usual system we employed to converse under the very noses of the policemen.

"That's rather a misfortune," he said.

"I'm sure it is," I answered.

"Well, I wish you the best."

That was September 27.

The next day, I waited for the moment I would be summoned for an investigation. But nothing happened. The twenty-eighth went by. The twenty-ninth arrived. The sun was setting earlier and earlier. The thirtieth, the last day of September, then October the first. It was beginning to be a little chilly in the evening; some clouds had gathered in the sky. The sun set at 6:04 that day. What would I do? How could I go and sign in at 6:00 and then go out for a walk when the sun had already set?

9
OCTOBER 2, 1969

The second of October came. I woke up as usual and
spent the morning reading . . . and thinking. At 1:00 I stepped
into the tavern, and then I saw the tourists! My eyes first fell
on the very long blonde hair of a tall and beautiful girl, and
a pair of bronze legs under a very short skirt. This was the
first miniskirt to appear on Amorgos! And then the whole picture took focus. Near her stood a man with a red beard and
a camera hanging from his shoulders, and another man was
sitting down. And then my eyes fell on . . . *The Tragedy of
Lyndon Johnson.* There was the book, all right. There were
four men and the young lady. I didn't look at them in any
special way. I went to my little table and sat down. The
gendarme was there having his meal at another table. The
airman had just finished eating and had left. The group was
talking French to Aspasia, rather good French I thought, be-

lieving I suppose that French is the language that would serve them best. But soon I heard them exchanging words in Italian among themselves and understood that they were genuine descendants of the Romans.

Aspasia had just placed before me my last *plat du jour* at her tavern. It was green beans of the brand known in Greece as vine-beans, which I didn't much like. Then I noticed that one of the Italians, who proved to be the chief of the operation, was looking at me rather intently, obviously wondering if I had understood who they were, if I was their man. He then picked up a straw hat and covered up the Lyndon Johnson book, which was lying on a chair near him. I was sitting in such a position that I could communicate with him by facial expression without being seen by the policeman. So I immediately gave a worried look because he had covered the book. He then uncovered it, and I immediately looked relieved. From that moment, they were sure I had understood, and that I was their man. I quickly finished my meal and left. They (as I heard later) had their lunch, then boarded the sole car on the island and went down to the port to leave. They had been through the village and visited the monastery in the morning, but I just hadn't happened to see them.

On the way down to the port, something they didn't like happened. One of the policemen got into the car with them and started asking why they had come there and what they had seen. But Anna, the woman, played her role beautifully, posing and flirting with the gendarme all the way. The ride is only seven kilometres, and they reached the port without having given anything away. They boarded the yacht and at about 3:30 P.M. left for the open seas. I suppose everything seemed to be all right to the policeman and to his chief, to whom he reported later.

Meanwhile I was very busy. This was my last day. I had planned and practised just what I would do every moment, from the time I returned from the tavern after having seen my rescuers to the moment I left. First of all I took a nice clean shave. The next step was burning papers. I didn't have very many papers that were in any way incriminating. A few notes I had kept and some texts and books I wanted to save I had sent home with my daughter on her last visit. But there were letters covering the last two months, letters that had gone through the censorship all right, other notes I had, and the famous computer copybook, which I wouldn't like to be found. The letters might be very innocent communications from friends or relatives, but because I had received them in the last few days they could be connected with the escape and thought to be in code. The people who had sent them might get into trouble. So I had to burn papers. Since burning papers can attract attention, I had thought over how I should do it.

Every second or third morning, at the time I did my household chores, I would wash the floor and dust, and I used to burn the papers that I had used in the toilet. I couldn't have just stuffed papers into the hole because it would get all plugged up. Once the escape plan got going, I burned these papers every two or three days at 3:00 P.M. Since I had done that about fifty times without attracting the attention of the police I figured I could burn these papers safely on the fifty-first day. So I burned my cleaning papers in the toilet and this time included all the others. I was sorry to burn the copybook, which had many interesting things in it, but I couldn't do otherwise.

Then came the time to set the automatic electricity gadget. It had three buttons. One you placed at the time it was then. It was 3:40. The second button you fixed at the time you wanted the light to go on. I put it at 6:30. The third one was for the time you wanted the light to go off. I put that at 10:30. I had tested this mechanism a number of times. Once when I had made a mistake, the whole thing went wrong and I got very uneasy. But by now I knew how it worked.

When this apparatus was first sent to me, I saw that I couldn't apply it to the regular light fixture in the centre of the ceiling; it could only be used with a light that got electricity from a plug. Fortunately, there were plugs in the house. But I didn't have a lamp. So quite openly, through the post, I asked my wife to send me the reading lamp from my study at home, saying I could not read very well with the ceiling light. The lamp arrived a fortnight later through the regular post as a parcel. Ever since, it had been that light which I had put on in the evening, so as not to create even a shade of difference in intensity for the guard to notice when I escaped. So for about two months before the escape, I had put on the desk light every evening, regardless of whether I was reading or working at the desk. As a matter of fact, I got up on a chair and took out the bulb from the central light fixture in case I forgot and put it on one evening.

After I had fixed the mechanism, I went through another procedure, which I think must have played an important role in gaining time for me. The house had four rooms, all in a row. I used only the first room, with a little kitchenette that was near it. The second, third, and fourth rooms had no furniture. The fourth room had one great advantage for my plans: it had no window. You could communicate with each room only by going through the previous one; there was no corridor. The gendarmes knew that I had my bed in the first room, which was my living room; but I moved my bed into the fourth room, the dark room, and arranged the first room in such a way that it appeared to be used only as a sitting room, a room where I could do my reading and writing and have my meals, a room where it would be logical to have the light on until 10:30. If all went according to plan and I was far away the next morning, the gendarmes would come to the house to see what was wrong when I didn't show up to sign in. Since the house was a second-floor apartment, they couldn't see directly in from outside. They would have to come up the outside staircase leading to my little veranda and knock at the door. They would get no answer. Then they would knock a second time and a third. I didn't think they would break the door down at that time, since there was always the possibility that I was asleep or sick, or that I might have died for that matter. I supposed they would take a ladder to look into the room from the window, which had no shutters. Fortunately, they could not get into the room through the window, because it had very heavy and narrowly spaced bars through which even a cat couldn't pass. They would look at the first room, see it in good order, and see no bed there.

"Ah," they would say, "he's obviously sleeping in another room; he has moved his bed."

They would never think that I had suddenly taken my bed on my shoulders, like another Lazarus, and marched through the village with it. They would take the ladder to the second room, which again had bars rather than shutters at the window. They would look in, and there would be an empty room. They would then take the ladder to the third room (or at least I supposed they would) and they would see another empty room. But then the fourth room had no window. Since the bed was not in the other three rooms, they very plausibly would think that I had moved my bed into the dark room, which was much warmer to sleep in, since winter was coming. Now what was I doing, they would wonder. Was I oversleeping? Was I sick? There was a good possibility that I was in there, since the bed had obviously been moved into that room.

So I moved the bed and arranged it as if it had just been slept in; as if I had gotten up early in the morning, leaving my pyjamas on top, and then I staged a joke, such as I had been yearning to do. I frequently had to resist the temptation to play some sort of joke on my guards. This one they would discover only when it would be too late for them to take it for an indication that I was trying to escape. On that bed, I placed a book of poems by our national poet, Dionysios Solomos, open at the page that contains a verse which reads:

> The day was late in coming,
> and all was quiet;
> under the shadow of threat,
> and the oppression of slavery . . . .

Then I locked that room, took the key with me, walked into the third room, locked it, took that key with me, walked into the second room, locked it, and finally arrived in the first room with all the keys in my hand. Some of these doors also had padlocks, and I used them, too. I thrust the keys deep into my pocket in case I had to return the next morning. Then I picked up the things I would need, the walkie-talkie, the flashlight, and a blazer which I would wear. I was then in my shirt sleeves since it was still quite warm. I locked the last room, went out onto the veranda, and very carefully looked to see if anyone was around, especially the guard up on the windmill. No one was there. I locked the entrance door, descended the staircase, and went into the primitive W.C.

There I left the walkie-talkie, the flashlight, and the blazer hidden behind a pail. The time was 4:50. I had to wait. I stood there for a while. At exactly 5:18 I started nonchalantly walking through the village. At 5:22—I had timed it all very meticulously—I entered the greengrocer's shop. I said, "Good afternoon," I asked for a few tomatoes, paid for them, took them in my hands, and went to the Gendarmerie to sign. But I always signed at 6:00, and it was only 5:29! That was the plan: I would go in and dare to sign half an hour earlier. There were three possibilities: first, the sergeant would not notice it was 5:30 and not 6:00; second, he would ask me to come back at 6:00 because it was not the right time to sign (they were rather particular about little things like that); third, I would walk in very quickly and, before the sergeant had the time even to look up, I would already have signed the book, which was always open on a table near him. Since the signature was in ink, the worst that could happen would be for him to tell me: "Well, please, next time, do come at exactly 6:00; it is only 5:30, and you're not supposed to sign that early."

But he couldn't erase my signature and have me come back at 6:00 because it was in ink. If I walked in rather slowly and had a little talk with him before I signed as I often did, he might very well tell me—politely perhaps—"Be so kind as to take a little stroll and come back at 6:00 because I want everything to be in order. You must sign at the given time."

I entered the office of the Gendarmerie holding my tomatoes, which I had bought purposely to show that I had come out for some other business and was using the occasion to come to sign. I rushed to the table and before the sergeant knew it I had already signed. But this movement didn't seem to impress him. He didn't look at his watch. He said nothing. Very likely he thought it was the proper time. When one has seen a man coming in and signing his name on time 816 times, one is not impressed. One doesn't look at the time anymore. Perhaps my precautions were a little exaggerated, but it is wise to make doubly sure about everything when a plan of escape is on.

By the way, the register in which I signed had many pages, with enough space for about twenty signatures per page. It was odd, but that last day I was signing on the last page of the copybook. As a matter of fact, I had remarked to the policeman that morning, "You'll have to prepare another register because there's space for only three more signatures."

"Oh, yes, I'll have to see to that," he had said.

As I was walking out of the office, the sergeant called me.

"Mr. Mylonas," he said, "I want you."

"That's odd," I said to myself. I came back, but was very calm.

"Your money has arrived," he said and handed me an envelope.

We were paid 17 drachmas a day by the government as an exile salary, which was paid at the end of every month. It being October 2, the September installment had just arrived. So I signed for it (therefore I was in good order with the dictatorship) and walked out. I don't think I ever walked to my house in such an innocent way. I crossed the street and said hello to the villagers, and walked at an easy pace back to my house. I had already planned that this walk would be rather slow.

The sun on that day set at 6:02. When I got home, it was 5:38. I immediately went to the toilet and picked up my things in order to depart. But what would I do with the tomatoes? I dumped them in a pail of soapy water that was in the W.C., the water I had washed in, since there was not enough water to flush it. The water was grey, and you couldn't see through it. But to my surprise, something I never thought of happened: the tomatoes floated! I did not want that indication of my movements to remain there. I did not have time to unlock the house and leave them in the kitchen, nor was it advisable for me to be seen unlocking the house with all those keys after all the pain I had gone to to lock it properly and secretly. I couldn't take them with me. In the end I hid them behind a bush in the little yard in front of my house.

But was I going to walk straight through the village holding a rather big flashlight and a walkie-talkie? Obviously not. For many days, I had been practising how to hide these things in front of my little mirror. One way was to have them sort of coiled up under my blazer. But that made it seem as if I were carrying a parcel of some sort, which was not very regular. So after many a test, I finally worked out what seemed the best way. I unbuttoned my shirt, put the walkie-talkie inside above my waist along my body, and did roughly the same thing with the flashlight, which was quite a big one. If someone looked at me carefully, he would see a big bulge under my trousers and my shirt, from my thigh nearly up to my neck. I couldn't walk out that way. So what I did was carry my blazer in a rather odd way in front of me with my hand covering it—not the usual way one carries a blazer. For two months before leaving, every evening when I went for my walk, I would take my blazer along, holding it in that odd fashion. If Mylonas was a little odd in the head and took his blazer for walks in that way, and did it for sixty-five days, it wouldn't impress anyone if he did it on the sixty-sixth. Throughout the hottest days of summer, when I really didn't need it at all, I would take the blazer with me; and I never forgot, when I reached my destination and sat down for a while, to throw it over my shoulders to show that I had some use for it. If they noticed that I was just carrying my blazer around for no obvious reason, the gendarmes would either think that I had gone crazy or that there was something mysterious going on.

I took one final turn at the lock on the door, another at the lock of the gate, and then out I went, strolling toward the exit of the village that I had picked for my last trip out of Hora. There were two or three ways of reaching the place I wanted to get to. Following careful observation, I had finally decided on a sort of middle course that would take me to the tree I mentioned before, and thence, ultimately, to my goal.

I hadn't walked more than fifty yards from my house when I met the doctor, who was probably a follower of the dictatorship. I hadn't seen him for about a month and a half because he had been on leave.

"Good evening, Mr. Mylonas. How are you? You're still here, poor fellow?"

And there I was, holding all my apparatus under my blazer, shaking hands with him, and saying, "Yes, and by the look of things, I think it will be one more winter here!"

"You're off on your evening walk?"

"Yes," I said, "it's always good for me. Good night."

"Good night."

And I casually walked out of the village. I suppose that the guard on duty that day must have been following me in the usual way, but I did not turn my back once. Anyway, it wouldn't have made much difference. He must have come to the end of the village as he usually did. When I had walked quite a bit away from the village, I used the classic method to look back by stooping and tying my shoe-lace, looking between my legs all the while. No one was following me. The guard had obviously stopped at his usual place. So from that point onward I walked at a quicker pace. I had not yet reached the place where it would be considered odd for me to be seen, when I saw a man on a mule coming toward me, returning from his fields. I soon recognised who he was, a good man, and one certainly against the dictatorship. This is the time to have another chat with the minister, he thought. He stopped, jumped off the mule, and started.

"Where will it end? How long will it go on? What do you think?"

He wanted a whole political analysis of the situation in Greece, and he brought in the Middle East, too. Time was passing. I must have spent about three or four minutes talking with him, which I could ill afford, but I wanted to seem as natural as I could. After a short talk, I told him that I had to be on my way because I wanted to walk a little that day. I had been reading all day long, I said, and it wasn't good for me not to walk. Another day, I promised, we would talk again. He didn't mind. He said good night, got on his mule to return to the village, and I proceeded on my way.

I was about to reach the tree, and I hadn't met anyone else. Immediately after I got to the tree I would start descending the path that I had never tried before. Then I saw two people on donkeys coming from afar. I bypassed the tree and continued as if to show that I was just walking on the level ground and didn't have any thought of going down toward the sea. The two people proved to be a woman and her son, a boy of about twelve. I knew who they were. It was about 6:25 by then, and the sun had well set. The first thing the woman said was, "Where are you going at this time? Isn't it a bit late for you to have your walk? You might stumble on a stone."

"I was a little late coming out tonight as I got absorbed in reading," I answered, "but I have to walk a bit," and I just walked past them.

But I didn't like that: me walking away from the village at that hour was news. When she got home, she would very likely tell her husband that she had seen Mylonas at 6:30 walking away from the village at quite a distance. They wouldn't be ill meaning, but by that evening everyone in the local café could be aware of the fact, and it might reach the ears of the police. The path they were taking back to the village mounted a bit at that place and had two curves. They were about to turn on the first curve and would therefore see me again. I sat down so that when they rounded the curve, with me well within view, they must have said: "That's as far as he goes; he's stopped to rest."

The moment they took the second curve, I got up and started walking back toward the village. From that moment I would not be news. To see Mylonas returning to the village at 6:30 was something that they saw practically every evening. Even if they said something, it would help my plan as "evidence" that I had returned. I waited until they vanished behind the hill, then turned back and started walking away again.

I found the path by the tree and started descending at a quick pace. From time to time I looked up to see if anyone was on the edge of the hill looking down. I put on my glasses to make quite sure, but there was no one. I am a little myopic and wear eyeglasses once in a while when I want to see far, but while in Amorgos I purposely never once used them, so that if one day I had to at a crucial moment—and this was one—it would be one more indication that this bespectacled man at a distance was not Mylonas, who never wore eyeglasses. It was getting darker and darker by now. The path very quickly disappeared; soon there was no path to speak of. But I soon found the manger, which was an old whitewashed structure. Next I had to find the dry bed of the stream. That wasn't easy since it had already gotten quite dark. I searched on the left, I searched on the right, and I could not find it. I was dripping with perspiration.

I suppose it was about five minutes in all—though it felt like a century—before I found the bed of the little rivulet. I started down along it immediately. It was a very capricious sort of stream, it turned and it hooked, it went right and left behind thorny bushes, it disappeared and appeared again; and I very faithfully followed it. Somewhere along the way I tore my trousers. Then suddenly I came to a point where in the winter it went into a graceful waterfall. I couldn't vault over the waterfall down into the bed of the stream, so I took a roundabout way, always keeping my eyes fixed on the rock from which the waterfall fell. I very nearly lost my way again, but I finally found the stream below the rock and continued down. When I think back on my escape, I always remember that last struggling and fighting contact I had with the Greek earth, with the fragrance of thyme and the feeling of the earth in my palms, and the smell of the sea already reaching me.

The sea seemed very near, perhaps because the terrain was so steep; but it wasn't. I was getting more and more careful because if I broke a leg or just sprained an ankle, I would have to stay there, and that would be the end of the escape. So it took me quite some time, and it wasn't until 7:20 that I at last reached the little bay. I looked up. It was pitch dark by then. Certainly no one could see where I was. I sat on the pebbles near the sea and washed my face with sea water. Then, though I thought that it was a bit early yet, I took the walkie-talkie out of my shirt. I put up the antenna, put it to my ear, and opened it to see if I could hear anything. What a coincidence and a relief! It was just the moment that they were making their first transmission from the ship. A voice was speaking English with an Italian accent in a way that seemed as if he wasn't expecting an answer.

"We're testing, we are testing, are you there? Over."

There they were! I pressed the button for me to talk.

"Yes," I said, "I'm here. I can hear you. I am ready. I am waiting. Over."

They were jubilant on the other side. I heard more voices. The walkie-talkie was clear enough. Later they told me how happy they had been that it worked so easily. They answered.

"We're coming. Be sure you wait for us. That's wonderful, congratulations."

And then the conversation went on and off, but there was a change in the voices: it was now good English with a rather American accent. I didn't understand who it was.

"We're about four miles away at sea," the voice said. "Can you hear our engine?"

I paused for a while, then answered, "'No, I can't. Over."

"Don't worry, it's because we're far. In a little while you'll start hearing it. Please tell us when you do. Over."

"Ah, I can now vaguely hear your engines," I said. "Over."

Well, it went on that way. The engines became clearer. They then told me they were about two miles away. Then I was told not to fret, that I would not hear the engines anymore because they would put them at a much lower gear in order not to create much noise.

A few minutes later I couldn't hear the engines. But then gradually, in the very dark night, I again heard the sound of a motor working very slowly—bop, bop, bop. It was at quite a distance still. Then the voice came again.

"We're not far now, about a mile away. We're approaching."

Then they asked me to use the flashlight, to put it on and off three times. I did.

"Don't you hear us?" they asked.

"Yes, I've done it," I said.

"We can't see it. Do it again."

I did.

"We can't see it."

I wondered what was wrong. Perhaps there was a rock that covered me. This lack of communication lasted for three or four minutes. We were a bit nervous on both sides.

Then at last they said, "Oh, we just saw the light. It's very very dim in the distance."

It seems that the light wasn't strong enough, which was just as well, because that meant that it couldn't be seen by anyone on top either. Not that there was anyone to see it, I suppose. I thought that by this time the electricity in my house would have been on for more than an hour. The guards would be guarding an empty house and all would be well. Then another order came over the walkie-talkie.

"From now on, please pay more attention to speed than to security. We have stopped." I really couldn't hear the motor anymore. "We're about to launch the dinghy. Will you please keep putting your flashlight on and off so that we know exactly where you are and can come directly toward you."

I started following their instructions, and suddenly, in that very quiet night, an infernal noise, or what I thought was an infernal noise, started up. It was the motor of the little rubber raft dinghy, as it turned out. It seemed to be a very strong motor, though in fact it wasn't. I thought that it would be heard all over Greece, not only in Amorgos! Brrrrrrrrrrrrrt. I flicked the flashlight and before I knew, the raft was in front of me. A voice asked me to walk into the sea. I went into the water knee-deep and I was pulled up on the raft. There we were, heading for the open sea.

In the darkness I recognised one of the Italians I had seen at noon, and then I turned around, and whom did I see? Elias, my son-in-law, in person! I was certainly happy to see him. He had decided to join the expedition, and he had chosen wisely. He knew the place, he was a Greek, he was a great help. He was really the chief of the whole operation, and thank God he was. With the troubles they had had on the way, I don't think they would have made it if hadn't been for his skillful and diplomatic leadership. Of course, he did not come out on the island or up to my village at noon, since he was known there. Early that morning, before landing in Amorgos, our Italian friends had left him on a barren rock of an island, where he had hid in a little cave with some food. They had picked him up at 5:00 the same afternoon. He had spent the whole day not knowing what was happening, whether they had seen me, whether they had been arrested, or what. He has since related to me how happy he was when he saw the ship heading for his little rock to pick him up and he was told by his fellow seamen, "It seems to be fine. The man saw us, and we hope that he will be there on time tonight." It was his voice I had heard over the walkie-talkie speaking in good English. I didn't exactly recognise it, but it had seemed vaguely familiar.

Well, we boarded the raft and raced to the open sea in complete darkness. As a matter of fact, for a moment Elias and his Italian partner couldn't locate the ship. It was about 500 metres from the coast, lying dead still without a light on. As I saw it, it appeared quite small. It was a cabin-cruiser, not much bigger than a big American car. We reached it and were pulled aboard and so was the raft, and before we knew it, the two motors were on and we were dashing away in the darkness of the night. I lost my equilibrium and fell, so quickly did the boat start. All the lights were off. I looked around and there were my friends, the "tourists" I had seen at noon, along with one more whom I hadn't met: he had remained in port with the little boat. And, of course, there was Elias. I sort of searched for the girl, but I didn't see her miniskirt or the blonde hair anymore. Being a woman, she had found the time to change attire! She was in blue jeans, and she was wearing a beret with her hair curled up under it and was helping the men with the ropes. At first when I entered, I thought there was a crew of seven men. I told her so, and she laughed. A little while after that, as the craft was speeding away in the night, she prepared some food for us. What else but Italian spaghetti!

I was very grateful to these people. The first thing I said when I had got aboard and sat down on a bench was *"Bon soir, mes amis."* They came up to me and, although they had never met me before, they all kissed me on both cheeks. That was Mediterranean warmth. I was then told who I was, because of course I was no longer George Mylonas. A false passport was waiting for me. I was a man of forty-eight, a citizen of another nation.* Unmarried, I was a bank accountant by profession. The height on the passport more or less corresponded to mine, and the color of my eyes did, too. I was asked to learn all that by heart. It's a good thing that the man was not married and didn't have any children. I wouldn't have too much to learn. Fancy me forgetting the name of my wife! I learned to copy his signature, because it was a real passport which had had the photograph changed and mine put in its place. I learned how to write that signature pretty well. It was an easy one, and I had to sign it twice later on.

---

* For legal reasons, I hesitate to mention the name of the nation.

Then I noticed that the navigator, the man with the red beard who had covered up the Lyndon Johnson book with his hat, had a very good map before him. He told me it was one of the maps used in the war by the Italian Naval General Staff, the Dodecanese then being Italian. We were near the Dodecanese. He had somehow managed to get hold of a map in Rome that showed practically every reef. It was pitch dark and the boat was certainly racing. Fortunately, we had no accident. Those were the waters in which the body of Nikiforos Mandilaras was found, the lawyer who tried to escape from the dictatorship and was killed.

Let me describe who my saviours were: the young girl was Anna—she worked in a fashion boutique in Rome; the man with the red beard, Mario Scialoja, was a journalist from the Italian magazine *Espresso*; there was Lorenzo, a lawyer from Rome; Giancarlo, an assistant university professor; Carlo, a university student; and one professional sailor, a good friend of theirs, from an Italian port. They were all under or around their thirties, progressives who hated dictatorships and rescued me for pure ideological motives.

The sea was very quiet. No winds blew. At about midnight, we came up against some trouble: a medium-sized ship with all its lights on was heading directly toward us. It could be a merchant ship or a destroyer; we didn't know what it was. It probably hadn't seen us, but we didn't know. With our lights out, the captain turned our boat ninety degrees, directing us to the left, far away from the other boat. A little later the ship went by the position where we had been, and we lost it to the south. It was probably never aware of our presence. But it was a tense moment, because we didn't know whether an alert for my escape had been given. Perhaps it hadn't been. The guards were probably watching the empty house, thinking I was sound asleep and everything was well in the village of Amorgos. But there was no way of knowing for sure.

At about 1:00, the moon came out, quite bright, almost a

full moon, lighting the sea. We could thus see a little better where we were going. We were heading for the straits between the island of Kos and the small island of Pserimos. About 2:00 A.M. we saw that there was a ship, bigger than ours, actually stopped in the middle of the entrance to the straits. I don't know how it happened, but we almost came up against it; it was too late to turn away, so the captain lit two lights, red and green, on the right and the left of the ship, and didn't try to hide our presence. They told me to hide in the keel behind a barrel, a place we had prepared earlier in case we were searched on the way. This would have worked only if it was a routine checking of passports. If they had some notion that I had escaped and a search was on, it would be relatively easy to find me in my hiding place. The Italians remained on deck as we came near the ship and asked in Italian the way to Kos, in order to say something. Those aboard the ship, being Dodecanese fishermen, knew some Italian and showed them the way. A little later I was asked to come up. I was told that it was a fishing vessel that had stopped in the middle of the sea and was fishing at night. That's why it had appeared to be blocking our way at the beginning of the straits.

We entered the straits between Kos and Pserimos, and a little later, we passed near the town of Kos, with its lights on. It was about 2:30. The noise of our engine must have been heard, but there didn't seem to be any problem. We must have been taken for a genuine tourist yacht.

Our destination was Turkey. Greeks and Turks have been traditional enemies for the last four hundred years. I certainly do not believe in that enmity any longer, and I look forward to the day when the two peoples, led by truly democratic governments, will become close friends and associates. However, in 1968 the situation was still tense, and landing on the Turkish coast was not an easy proposition for a Greek.

To begin with, you had to have a Turkish visa, which was usually not granted. Then, in view of the semi-totalitarian régime in Turkey, there was a good chance I could be handed back to the Junta, with whom the Turkish Government was on good terms. That was the reason I bore a non-Greek passport.*

We wanted to reach the port of Bodrum, the former Greek city of Halicarnassus in Asia Minor. As we were heading for Bodrum during the night, I told my Italian friends, "Do you know what Bodrum means in Turkish?" They didn't know. I said, "Prison."

"That's not a very good omen," they replied.

It seems there was a fortress in Bodrum that was used as a prison in the old days, and that's how the town got its name.

We passed Kos without any trouble. We had heard that Greek torpedo boats were on patrol in the straits between Kos and Turkey. But we were lucky enough to pass at a moment when a patrol vessel was not in evidence. I can still remember the glee of the Italian captain when he shouted, checking his map and looking at me, "Gentlemen, I can now tell you we are safely in Turkish waters."

What an irony for a Greek to be safer in Turkish than in Greek waters.

---

* It should be recalled that George Panagoulis (a third brother of Alexander Panagoulis), an army officer, had managed to escape to Israel, where he was handed over to the Greek authorities. His end was tragic: he jumped (or was he pushed?) into the sea from the ship that was bringing him back to Greece, and was drowned.

10
FREE

Bodrum is located deep in a sort of fjord, in Asia Minor. The whole trip was about ninety nautical miles from Amorgos. From the moment we entered Turkish waters, we felt rather safe, because we were sailing at night with Turkish coasts on both sides as we went deeper and deeper into the bay. It was about 4:00 A.M. when we saw the lights of Bodrum. When we came into port, no one seemed to take notice of us; we found a place to moor our boat without any trouble. When daytime came, we saw we had actually moored alongside a torpedo boat of the Turkish Navy, and an armed sailor was mounted guard on its deck. But in the dark early hours of the morning no one seemed to be around. We actually jumped ashore. I'm sure we could have entered a car, if it had been prearranged, and left for the interior of Turkey without any-one's being the wiser; but the idea was to enter Turkey officially with stamps on our passports so that when we left (which I hoped would be quite soon) we would be in good order. It was decided therefore that we would all remain on the boat and try to sleep. I don't think anyone really did.

At about 5:00 A.M. Elias got out. He told us then that, in view of the fact that we were not at all sure what kind of reception we would get from the Turkish authorities, he had taken certain precautions. There was the danger that we might simply be told to leave, which would really put us on the spot: where could we go, with Greek waters surrounding us? And what if the Junta had raised the alarum for me and claimed I was a common criminal? The Turks could have arrested me. Elias had therefore arranged, through the kind intermediary of a Greek lady living abroad, to contact a diplomat from a friendly European nation, who was waiting for us in Bodrum and had been for more than a week, we later found out. If anything went wrong with the Turkish authorities when we went through passport control, he would appear to say that his government had undertaken to give me political asylum. So Elias went to find this man.

There were two hotels in Bodrum, the Hotel Halikarñassos and the Hotel Artemis. There had been some misunderstanding as to which hotel the foreign diplomat would be staying at. When Elias got to the first hotel, there was no concierge. He went in and saw a series of rooms where people were obviously sleeping. He just couldn't go knocking at every room at 5:00 A.M., so he left. At the other hotel he found someone who didn't seem to be aware of the presence of our man on the premises. So Elias came back, but the trip had taken him quite some time and we were anxious. At about 7:00, Elias went out again and finally located the diplomat. We'll call him Peter.

Peter said: "At 8:00, when the office opens, you disembark, all of you, pass through customs, and have your passports stamped. I will be strolling around outside. You will pretend not to know me and I in turn will pretend not to know you, but I'll be around. If anything goes wrong, you just approach me."

We followed his instructions, transmitted to us by Elias. In the meanwhile, the town and port were waking up. People were going around, all Turks—I don't think I saw any other nationality there—talking loudly, like the Greeks. And then we saw a tall, young, fair man strolling up and down the embankment.

"He's the man, the diplomat," Elias told me.

As had been agreed, we didn't talk to him. At last, a little after 8:00, the customs and passport office opened. A rather lazy employee looked at our passports. I don't know why, but my Italian friends, who up to then had been quite calm during this daring operation, got quite nervous. First, the captain of the ship was asked to show the ship's documents, which were not found to be in completely good order. Finally, after some discussion, they said it was all right. He was then asked to say from what Greek port he was coming. He said Kos, which was not true, but it was rather doubtful that they would check on that. And then they took ages going through the passports of my friends. Elias had his regular American passport, though he had used another one while in Greece. The amusing part was that while I was the only real suspect, perhaps because I was older and more respectable looking, the Turkish policeman just glanced at my passport, stamped it, said "*Merci, Monsieur*" in Turco-French, and gave it back to me immediately. Mine took about ten seconds, while all the others had their passports kept for nearly five minutes each!

After that we were supposed to go through customs. We were asked to go and bring our luggage. I had nothing with me, but then Elias gave me a valise.

"This is yours," he said.

"What's in it? I asked.

"It's really yours," he said. "There's some clothing of yours in it."

So I took my valise. They opened up everything, didn't find anything irregular, and we thought we were through. But we still had to go through a medical examination before entering Turkey. The doctor was not to be seen. About an hour later, at about 10:00, a rather fat Turk turned up; he was the doctor. He didn't examine us. He just took our passports and put a seal on them, which obviously meant "healthy" in Turkish, and we were through at last. We had officially, legally, and properly entered the territory of the Turkish Republic.

After that, we actually spoke to Peter. He said he had a car bearing Izmir licence plates that he had rented in Izmir. It was a grey Volkswagen. He said he was ready to take me and whoever wanted to come along to Smyrna, which the Turks today call Izmir.*

Mario Scialoja of *Espresso*, Elias, and myself entered the car. The other three would go by local bus to Smyrna, and the remaining two would stay on the boat and start sailing north, without entering Greek territorial waters, following the coast of Asia Minor from Bodrum into Smyrna harbour. The plan was that in Smyrna, the boat, which was quite small, would be loaded on a regular merchantman and shipped back to Italy. So we parted there. I expressed my gratitude to five of these people who had come to help me: I saw them much later in Italy. The four of us, Peter, Elias, Mario, and myself, entered the Volkswagen, and off we went.

It was about 10:15, and by then I was wondering what would be happening in Amorgos. They must have found out. Nine o'clock had gone by, and I hadn't reported to sign. Perhaps they had given me a little leeway, but by about 9:30

---

* Smyrna was also at one time a flourishing Greek city. In 1922 it was partly destroyed during the Asia Minor débacle of the Greek Army.

the whole thing must have exploded. But I didn't think of that very much. As a matter of fact, I had quite a tourist-like feeling that morning, after having been secluded on the island for so long. It was the first time I had set foot in Asia Minor. It reminded me very much of Greece. The road was a good old macadam road, but well preserved. Pine trees, olive trees, fig trees, and once in a while, an ancient Greek temple and ancient Greek wall—I really felt very much at home. On the way, I began giving all sorts of historical information to my friends. We passed near the renowned ancient Greek city of Ephesus; the Turks call it Efes today. I told them stories about the Graeco-Turkish war of 1922. We saw the track of the Aidinion Railway from which part of the Greek Army and hinterland population had reached Smyrna during the débacle. All this was very moving for me. For a while I forgot my own experiences and concentrated on what I saw. But time was getting on. Peter said we were due to take a plane out of Izmir to Istanbul at 2:00. He thought it was impossible for us to reach the plane on time, since it had taken so much time to go through passport control and customs. But the Greek in us, not always the most conformable of spirits, spoke up. Both Elias and I said, "Oh, we'll make it," and we asked the man at the wheel to step on the gas and dash for Smyrna. And so he did. We reached the city at 1:50; the airfield was a few kilometres away on the opposite side of town. We stopped briefly in the city. Elias was to stay there to help the Italians send the ship back to Italy, and he kept the car to return it to the renting office so that no precious time would be lost by Peter.

How well Elias had organised everything. After having failed to get help in Cyprus and Lebanon three months earlier, he had gone to Italy, where he met a Greek doctor who had previously been introduced to him in Switzerland by a Greek lady who fights the Colonels very actively and loves liberty. Through the doctor, he contacted a group of young men connected with the progressive side of the Italian political spectrum, and told them of our plan. He did not mention whom they would rescue, nor to what island they would have to go. Finally, after about a month of discussion, it was agreed that a boat would be provided by our Italian friends at the port of San Stefano, south of Rome, on the Tyrrhenian Sea. The group that ultimately came to Amorgos was gradually formed by volunteers; no one accepted a cent for his services. They met Elias, who didn't give his real name, and they started in the first days of September in order to make it for the eleventh, as had been agreed. But they were not more than fifty miles out of San Stefano when the motor broke down, and they had to go back, towed by another ship. It took them days to repair the motor. It was then that I got the first message from Eleni, who had remained in Athens, that the escape wouldn't be on the eleventh of September but on the nineteenth.

Then they started again. They reached their first Greek island, Corfu, where they stayed for a day. They sailed down the Ionian coast in Greek waters, and very near the small island of Paksi the motor broke down again. When they stopped at Paksi, Elias and one of the Italians went to Corfu. They couldn't find the necessary spare parts for repairs, so the Italian took an airplane from Corfu to Athens. Elias didn't go because it would have been dangerous. The next day the Italian returned to Corfu with the necessary materials, went to Paksi in a caique, repaired the boat, and they were on their way again after having lost four precious days. They sailed to the Gulf of Corinth and passed through the Corinth Canal. In the meanwhile, they were again late for their rendezvous with me. It was then I had received the second message from Eleni, saying she could not give me a specific date anymore, and I would have to wait for the book signal. It will be remembered that on September 25 there was a very rough sea. They had just entered the Aegean Sea and left the island of Aegina, when they came up against a big storm which the little ship couldn't face. For a whole day and night, they had taken refuge on a little, barren, uninhabited island: Aghios Georgios. They were not alone: a Greek merchant vessel was there taking shelter, too.

When the weather cleared they sailed for Paros. There they were nearly arrested. No one spoke Greek except Elias, but they forgot to be careful. Because of Elias, they had tuned on the radio to hear the weather bulletin in Greek. A policeman going by the harbour thought he heard them speaking Greek, although it was actually the radio; he denounced them for posing as foreigners. All seven were asked to report to the police.

"We know you're Greeks. Why do you conceal your identity?" they were asked.

Elias and his friends kept their sangfroid and, after showing their passports, explained that they had tuned into a Greek radio station for music, which had ended, and the speaker was saying something in Greek which the policeman had obviously heard. They were finally permitted to leave.

The next day they went to the island of Ios; and the day after that they came to pick me up. It is interesting that after Paksi the engine never broke down again, although they had rough seas, and it was only after we reached the coast of Turkey that they told me about their tribulations. They were terribly afraid it might break down in the midst of the straits we were crossing on the night of the escape. They had plenty of fuel on board, more than the tank could hold, and they had bought fuel at every stop on the way. They told me that in every island they stopped, the harbour master had wanted to know their previous port, which was obviously checked, as well as their destination. They always told the truth, so after they left Ios, they said they were on their way to Amorgos. It was the right thing to do, because when they reached Amorgos, the harbour master at Katapola again visited the ship and asked the usual questions. The only lie they ever told was when they informed the Turkish officer that they were coming from Kos.

Back to Smyrna now: to save time, we hailed a taxi, a big car with a powerful engine, a 1950 Chevrolet. The driver reminded me very much of the provincial Greek drivers. So the three of us, Mario, Peter, and myself, got into that car and we told him in English, French, or Italian to rush to the airfield. We didn't speak any Greek for obvious reasons, though it is known in that area; you can get around with Greek very well. On the way to the airport, the two foreigners were wondering if we were on the right track.

"For sure," I said.

"How do you know?" they asked. "It's the first time you've been here."

"I can see the signs," I said.

"But they're in Turkish."

"We understand a number of Turkish words because we have lived near each other for so long." The word was *hava-alani*. *Hava* in Turkish means "air" and *alan*, "square." They are both words that in other contexts are used in Greek, so I said to myself *hava-alani* is the air square, presumably the airport. And I was sure that we were on the right road.

We arrived at the airfield the moment the plane had started its motors. It was a Turkish National Airlines jet, with a red crescent and star on it. We rushed to the desk and told the girl we wanted to go to Istanbul.

"It's all right; the plane will wait," she said.

She checked the tickets. We boarded the plane just as they were closing the doors. It was about 2:15 on October 3. Twenty-four hours before I had just finished lunch in Amorgos, returned home, and started to burn my papers.

The plane was on its way to Istanbul. In a moment we heard

the voice of the captain saying: "Far to the left, you can see the Greek island of Mytilene."

We didn't exactly love that idea. If something happened to the plane and it landed on a Greek airfield, we wouldn't have gotten very far. But a little while afterwards we were flying over the Hellespont. History again began haunting me; it was the first time I had seen these places. The historic Gallipoli Peninsula, and a little later we were landing in the former capital of the Byzantine empire: Constantinople. We got out. There was no checking; it was an internal airline. It took us a little time to collect our light luggage. The plan was to go to a hotel in Istanbul, and not circulate about at all; at least, I wouldn't leave the hotel. The next day we would fly out. But it was only about 3:30 P.M. "Why not try and get out of here right away," I proposed. So the three of us, Peter, Mario, and myself, went to the desks of the different air companies. I think the first one was Alitalia.

"Do you have a flight out of Istanbul this afternoon?"

"Certainly, gentlemen," said the girl.

"What exactly is the itinerary?"

"Well, the plane leaves at 5:00 and it touches down in Athens and then goes on to Rome."

"Thank you; we'll come back later; we'll see."

We certainly didn't plan on landing in Athens. Then we went to Swissair.

"What do you have out of here right now?"

"What a pity," said the attendant, "ten minutes ago, a direct flight to Zurich left."

If we had been a little quicker, I would have reached Switzerland before twenty-four hours had elapsed from the moment I left Amorgos! But she continued, "It doesn't matter. There's another plane going to Geneva, with a stop in Athens."

We again thanked her very much but said we would think it over, we had not decided yet. Then we went to Air France.

Mario in the meanwhile had second thoughts, and he was right.

"Why shouldn't I go even if it stops in Athens? They don't know anything about me," he whispered. He bought a ticket and left for Rome, via Athens, that very afternoon.

The girl at the French desk said, "If you want to leave a litte later"—that was the excuse we gave—"why don't you try Olympic next door?"

We smiled very graciously and left. She smiled back with a question mark on her face. . . . We saw that there was no flight out of Istanbul that afternoon but via Athens. So we decided to stay. We booked tickets for a direct Swissair flight to Zurich the next morning at 9:00.

Peter and I decided to go to the city: not for sightseeing, certainly. Going through Smyrna might have proven dangerous, too, because it is a NATO base and there are a number of Greek officers stationed there. Someone might have recognised me. Though the way we dashed through that city and changed from the Volkswagen to the taxi almost excluded that possibility. Of course there was a chance that a Greek officer might be at the airfield or in the airplane. We decided to be cautious and take a taxi into Istanbul, not the airport bus. The taxi driver was very talkative and asked us our nationality. We said we were Americans. We told the taxi driver that both of us were visiting Istanbul for the first time. He very obligingly started showing and explaining monuments to us in broken English. I must say I was quite moved to be in that position; it was frustrating not to be able to express myself, not to be able to stop. He showed us the Byzantine walls and then he said, "This church is"—and he said it in Greek—"Aghia Sofia."

To a Greek it means a lot. I was impressed. We saw it at a distance. It was the big cathedral of the Byzantine emperors, built in 537 A.D. under Justinian. It became a Turkish mosque after the occupation of Constantinople in 1453, but lately it has had the status of a Greek Orthodox church-museum, without any services being held in it. My thoughts went to my paternal grandmother, who had spent about half her life here. Istanbul struck me as a beautiful but untidy and rather dirty city: it reminded me of Athens in the mid-forties; and that was familiarly pleasant to me.

We had told the driver to take us to the Istanbul Hilton: some change from my Amorgos "palace." We entered the Hilton, but let me remind my readers how I looked: I was wearing a blazer with holes in its two elbows; my trousers had torn as I was coming down the rocks; I hadn't shaved for more than twenty-four hours; and I don't think I exactly gave the impression that I was a typical Hilton customer. But as we came in, to play it safe, we began speaking enthusiastically about the wonderful hiking we had done on the mountain (whichever mountain that was!). So the clerk must have thought we were good rich bourgeois who were returning from an excursion. We chose the Hilton because one can be more easily lost in a big hotel like that. We took two rooms, high up, on the sixth or seventh floor. I was soon in a wonderful hot bath, the first one in a year and a half!

This is about the place where I suppose I should write something about "how unbelievable it was." Well, I didn't feel that way. I thought it very natural, as if I hadn't been out of a better life for more than a day or two. One quickly gets used to good things and easily forgets bad ones.

I didn't have any shaving equipment with me. My daughter had forgotten to put it in the valise she prepared for me. I shaved with Peter's shaver. It was an old-style one, and since I had been using an electric shaver for years, I cut myself badly. I got out my suit and a nice clean shirt, but there was no tie in the valise. It was summer, and Peter had only one tie with him. Then I looked at my shoes. I was still wearing the mountain boots I wore for walks on my stony island; they, too, had suffered from the descent the previous night. The heel of my left boot had remained on the cliffs of Amorgos. These certainly were not the shoes for me to go to the Hilton restaurant in. There were no socks in the valise either. I was wearing heavy woollen socks with big holes in them. I had to look respectable. So Peter actually locked me in my room and went out, taking the key with him. We were so near the end of our tribulations that he wanted to play it safe. It seemed ages before he came back. He returned with a pair of shoes in my size, a pair of socks, and a tie. All dressed up, nice and clean and shaven, and with me wearing eyeglasses, we went to the roof garden of the Hilton, and did we order a meal! I hadn't had a bite for the last thirty hours except for the spaghetti that Anna had prepared the night before on the boat. We ordered the best there was. I had no money with me. I naturally didn't dare produce the little Greek money that had been paid to me a few minutes before I took my leave from the sergeant; but Peter took care of these things. It seems we ate so much that when we ordered the third course, the headwaiter very politely told us in English, "You know, sir, this is not a dessert; this is another main course."

"Yes, yes, we know. Bring it along, please."

"As you like," he said. And turning around, he gave the order to one of the waiters . . . in Greek!

After having really enjoyed this excellent food, we went to our rooms and I lay down on that luxurious bed. Quite a new feeling after the wooden planks of my Amorgos bed. I didn't go to sleep very quickly—I never do anyway—but at last I dropped off, and I dreamed of a most casual day in my boyhood at home.

What was happening in Amorgos in the meanwhile? Much later, through bits of information that have reached me from time to time throughout the last two years, I gradually put together the following general picture.

FREE   183

The gendarmes actually broke into my house at about 11:00 A.M. They searched for me in all the rooms. They did not take any notice of the book with the national anthem, nor did they notice the automatic device that put the light on and off, which I had purposely concealed behind some papers. At about midday a meeting took place at the Gendarmerie. They were afraid to inform their superiors in Thira, let alone Athens, and they decided to launch a search in the village and its outskirts with the policemen bearing arms. I have been told that the exiled airman played his role beautifully by saying, when interrogated, that he thought I had appeared very melancholic recently and might have committed suicide in some deserted spot. And then, of course, there was always the possibility that I had suffered a heart attack. By early afternoon the Thira headquarters were informed. Papadopoulos himself was told I had disappeared, by a trembling Minister of Public Order, at about the time I was having my wonderful meal at the Istanbul Hilton! When night came the searching stopped. My house, with its broken doors, was guarded by two sentinels, who must have had the shivers when the light went on suddenly in my room! Was it a ghost? It was the automatic device which worked on a twenty-four-hour basis if not disconnected.

The next day the search continued, and a detachment of two officers and twenty-five armed policemen set sail in a caique from Naxos, in order to comb the whole island; they thought that I was probably still hiding on it. But Poseidon seemed to be on our side: the sea became so rough that the caique was obliged to take shelter for twenty-four hours on the little island of Donousa. When the detachment arrived in Amorgos, the population was almost certain that I had escaped, and watched with irony and inner satisfaction the "mopping up" operations of the Gendarmerie throughout the entire island. These abruptly stopped when, to the secret joy of my friends in Amorgos, the German radio announced that I had safely arrived "somewhere in Western Europe."

Back in Istanbul now: at about 6:00 A.M. Peter knocked at my door. We got up, had our breakfast, ordered a taxi, and out we went to the airport. We passed through customs and passport formalities. No one ever suspected that the passport wasn't really mine. . . .

The Swissair plane, a plane that I have since used many times, bearing the flag of a country that I have come to love, was there standing before the air terminal. A little while later, the flight was called, a direct flight to Zurich. We boarded it after checking once more to make sure that it was a direct flight. This was October 4, the second day after I had left Amorgos. By now I was sure the officials of the Junta in Athens would know. I smiled within myself. Had the news got out? Was there any mention of my escape on the foreign radio? I wondered. We boarded the plane and it started.

"We are now flying over Sofia, the capital of Bulgaria, which is to be seen at our left," the captain announced about twenty minutes later.

I touched elbows with Peter and whispered, "Happily, to the left," because if Sofia was to the right, we could very well be travelling over Greek Thrace and Macedonia. A little later, the voice of the captain announced that we were flying over Belgrade. Then, and only then, we knew that we had made it, because even if the plane had some engine trouble and had to land, it would not land on Greek soil. Alas, the country that had once been the cradle of liberty was no longer free; fortunately it was far behind!

At about 10:30 Swiss time, we came down at the Kloten Airfield in Zurich. Again, I was pleased, but I felt that what was happening was just to be expected. I didn't have that feeling of "pinch me because I don't believe it's true!" I don't know why I felt that way, but perhaps since I had planned it so meticulously and for so long, and because I was so sure that I would succeed in the end, the whole thing had a familiar touch about it.

We went through the transit room and a little later boarded another plane, to Geneva. At 11:45, October 4, 1969, I was in Geneva. At 11:45, October 2, 1969, I hadn't even known that my friends had come for me on Amorgos. That was quick work.

11
THOUGHTS
AND PROSPECTS

From the first moment I landed in Switzerland, two feelings were predominant in me. One was the lively feeling that as
an individual, as a citizen, I was a free man in a free country.
I did not need to whisper and look right and left. The dark
shadow of martial law did not reach me anymore. I could say
who I was and speak my mind. This is a feeling which is perhaps incomprehensible to those who have not experienced the
sour taste of a fascist dictatorship.

But on the other hand, I could not for a moment forget that
the Greek people were still suffering under the dictatorship's
yoke. My feeling of responsibility as a political and resistance
leader prevailed, and soon my initial feeling of liberty became
something outside my world, something for which I was grateful but which was far from being enough. I couldn't feel free
if Greece wasn't.

Never for a moment had I thought of escaping only in order to liberate myself. I escaped in full consciousness that coming abroad meant much tiresome, sometimes frustrating, and always hard work for the restoration of liberty in my country. My escape had one meaning for me from the start: to carry on the fight to liberate Greece from the curse which lies on it. And to explain to the European peoples with all means in my power that the neo-fascist fire that started on the Greek bridgehead can well spread to the whole of Europe if nothing is done to oppose it.

I was no longer an exile in Amorgos. But I was an exile abroad, along with a few hundred other Greeks. . . . Like them, I felt and continue to feel that I am burdened with a heavy weight of obligation and duties. We all have the primary duty to unite and help organise the liberation of the Greek people.

For a few weeks the international press gave great prominence to my adventure, and literally hundreds of people came to see me, telephoned me, wrote to me, welcomed me. I barely managed to cope with all that flow of communication (though, of course, I was grateful for it). I think my first period abroad was one of the most tiring in my life.

It is now three and one-half years since I escaped, and the dictatorship will soon celebrate its sixth anniversary. I will not dwell on the story of these years. It is contemporary Greek history and it is the history of Greek politics and resistance abroad. I am far too involved in this movement to be able to write about it at this time. I hope that one day the events of those years will be included in the first chapters of another book: *The Liberation of Greece.* Nor is it wise now to describe, praise, criticise, or attack my fellow Greeks who are carrying on the same struggle as I am. They belong to all political shades, they have their own philosophy and methods of action. They are all sincere; and they are, as a whole, trying their best. The future will prove who had the greatest foresight. And then, as I have repeatedly stressed in press conferences throughout Europe and the United States: "In matters of resistance secrecy is preeminent. The operation takes place first; the communiqué is issued afterwards."

The Swiss Government was kind and understanding. It officially granted me the status of a political refugee and gave me political asylum and the passport that goes with it. The authorities of the canton and state of Geneva have given me hospitality in their beautiful city. With Geneva as my base, and in my capacity of former member of Parliament and cabinet minister, and political spokesman of Democratic Defence, I have travelled all over Europe and the United States, I have spoken to prime ministers, ministers, members of Parliament, diplomatic officials, United Nations people. I have given about two hundred press conferences, speeches, radio and television broadcasts, been on panel discussions, written articles, given interviews, spoken to students, professors, workmen, ecclesiastic leaders. I officially testified against the dictatorship before the Council of Europe, together with C. Karamanlis, A. Papandreou, and C. Mitsotakis, on the morning of December 13, 1969. That afternoon the Colonels were ousted from the Council of Europe.

The fight is a hard one, and probably a long one, but I feel sure that the dictatorship will ultimately be overthrown. And I do not believe Papadopoulos will last as long as Franco has in Spain or Salazar in Portugal. But it is not enough just to believe it; there is still much that has to be done if we are not to undergo the fate of the two unfortunate Iberian peoples. I have recently been reading an interesting book about Portugal by a distinguished Portuguese exile. It is amazing how similar the methods of oppression and terrorism are; similar, too, are the idealism, mistakes, visions, and delusions of the anti-dictatorial forces!

Democracy is facing a crisis the world over. Totalitarian

régimes are in power in a great number of nations. The whole of Africa and South America, with very few exceptions, the greater part of Asia, and about half of Europe are under the dictatorships of the Eastern, Western, or Third World brands. If one were to count how many totalitarian régimes exist today, the list would be a very long one. I have calculated that out of the 3,419,000,000 inhabitants of our planet (1971 estimate), 2,324,000,000 live under dictatorial régimes of one kind or another. Those living under democratically elected governments amount to barely 1,095,000,000, and if it weren't for India's 547,000,000 inhabitants, this figure would have been just over 500,000,000. But isn't it a coincidence that those countries which still practice democracy within their borders are the leading powers in the civilisation of the world?

There are many explanations for this great surge of totalitarianism all over the world. It is a historic fact that democracy, in the last analysis, is the strongest and most durable system of government; but it has, by definition, the weakness of permitting all sorts of totalitarian-minded political minorities to express themselves and, many a time, to organise coups and seize power before the democratic majority has had the time to react. Once this minority, or clique of power-hungry, money-thirsty, political and military adventurers gets entrenched it is extremely difficult to get rid of it. Modern technology in the hands of the few who manage to run the government is powerful enough to keep down a whole people without much difficulty. When George Orwell wrote *1984*, he might have been thought to exaggerate. Today, perhaps he could be accused of not having had enough foresight! As a result of technological progress, privacy is jeopardised; the state can enter a private citizen's house, tap his telephone, and invade his inner thoughts, and awareness of this power is something that helps dictatorships and intimidates the people enormously.

Technological development is also responsible for the appalling increase in armaments: "progress" in methods of killing. We have now reached the point where huge sums of money are being spent annually throughout the world, but especially by the two super powers, according to the absurd rationale (which might perhaps have had some meaning in the days of the bow and arrow): "If you want peace, you should prepare for war." As it has been so correctly said recently: "If you want peace, you should *prepare for peace*." The industrial interests that are automatically linked to the enormous war machine are also totalitarian-minded. But then, is the United States a totalitarian nation? I do not believe it. Yet the "military-industrial" establishment of that country (the expression was coined by President Eisenhower) is very much connected to the interests of war, and war necessitates totalitarian methods. One thing we can say is that while the United States is not a totaliarian state within its own borders, it supports fascist totalitarianism and corrupt régimes the world over, and undermines democratic progressive régimes (as the C.I.A. and I.T.T. did in Chile) in order to advance the aims of its ruling establishment, although these aims do not basically coincide with the interests of the American people.

How many times have I heard the view that the best way to teach people to live under a real democracy is by imposing a dictatorship on them, a dictatorship which will train them to be good citizens of a democracy! This utter nonsense has been repeatedly proclaimed throughout the world and, of course, is gospel truth in Greece right now. It always reminds me of the simile coined by the Greek sociologist, George Skliros: "It is like trying to teach someone how to swim without letting him enter the water."

The question that could be asked at this point is: but are all dictatorships the same? Aren't some worse than others? Some dictatorships do represent a political movement that has the support of a segment of the population. Most of the Communist dictatorships fall into this general category; some of the Arab and African nationalist dictatorships do also. And we must admit that Mussolini's, Hitler's, and Franco's dictatorships to a certain extent fitted this description during their early years. But other dictatorships—the worst—are instituted by a small number of self-interested, ruthless individuals who are closely connected to, or are out-and-out organs of, foreign imperialistic and oligarchic interests, and who have no popular following. Haiti and most of the South American juntas, as well as the Greece of Papadopoulos, qualifies in this group. Some dictatorships have their origins in popular and/or nationalist revolutions. Who didn't want to do away with the corrupt reactionary régimes of Louis XVI, Tsar Nicholas II, or King Farouk? But were the ideals of these revolutions ultimately well served by the imperialistic wars of an absolute monarch, Napoleon? And were the prisons, the concentration camps, and the execution of hundreds of thousands by Stalin an improvement? Hasn't the personal dictatorship of Nasser ultimately proven to be narrow-minded and anti-progressive? That's one of the traps that revolutions fall into, especially in underdeveloped nations today: totalitarian régimes which, after becoming well entrenched, end up as ends in themselves, cut off from their roots of popular origin. That is why I adamantly and logically maintain that a dictatorship is always bad; even if it starts with the best of intentions, it always ends up by betraying its initial aims.

Am I over-optimistic when I say that I believe the outlook for democracy is a good one? There isn't a totalitarian country that doesn't face problems with its liberal-minded citizens. Reaction to totalitarian methods has set in, and our great hope lies in the young rising generations, whether in Spain, Russia, Iran, Czechoslovakia, Greece; or the United States, for that matter. But let those generations also beware the great temptation of totalitarianism. Let them never forget history's lesson, that the best way to run any country (if and when they come to power) is by applying truly democratic methods. May those young men and women who, in good faith, advocate the necessity of a new totalitarian state in order to do away with present-day dictatorships or reactionary capitalist democracies not end by setting up another form of terror-state. The idea is "not to change tyrants; it's to do away with tyranny."

Respect for human life is something that is certainly lacking in present-day world leaderships. There were terrible wars in the past, during times considered less civilised, but the complete disregard of human life which exists today in our twentieth-century civilised world is frightful. In the past, leaders of nations or their representatives who were to meet and decide about an armistice or a peace, took days and days to get to their meeting place. But once they got there, they usually sat down, discussed things, and reached some agreement within a logical period of time. Today, they rush to the site of the meeting in jets and then take weeks and months and years to discuss without reaching agreement, while daily receiving bulletins that report the number of dead on the battle-field. People get killed while governments talk. Did it never occur to the governments represented at the Paris-Vietnam peace talks (which took four years) that every time they met, to fool around once a week with phrases, denunciations, and propaganda, they had lost, between them, something like a thousand more citizens?

Today the leadership of the world, with some rare exceptions, is in the hands of mediocrities. Perhaps that's one of the explanations of why things are permitted to just drag along. Events take their course, and the leaders follow them; initiatives that could well change the trend of history seem to be strangely lacking. The world is led by technocrats and bureaucrats, rather than statesmen. There are still a few statesmen around, not at the head of the super powers unhappily, but they quite rightly feel they are not being understood. Nearly all their colleagues speak on another wave length!

How and when the Greek people are liberated from the present yoke cannot and must not be described here. Once it's done, however, we will fight for the establishment of a full-fledged democracy. This means that power goes to the people and derives from them. They will be the supreme masters; the government will represent them, their wishes and aspirations. They will make the laws under which they wish to be governed, and they will respect these laws. Freedom will exist in all spheres of life, and political democracy will be practised to its fullest extent.

Is what is called "formalistic democracy" enough? Certainly not. But only a democratic form of government will permit authentic democracy to prosper. Without the form we cannot reach the substance. Economic democracy goes hand in hand with political democracy. By economic democracy, I mean true socialism; I don't mean totalitarian socialism, but democratic socialism, socialism "with a human face." Has it been applied anywhere successfully? I can only say that some countries are heading in the right direction. The true socialist state will use the extraordinary power of present-day technology for the well-being of all its citizens, without distinction. All big industries, banks, communications, power plants, etc., must be public enterprises; a full medical and social security system, covering everyone without exception from cradle to grave, must be applied. Individual initiative can and must remain in a number of fields, but it must never become a monopoly of power. Education should really become universal, rationalised, modernised, and humanised, and given top priority in the Greece of tomorrow; and the way to live within a democratic state will be part of that education. The armed forces, for as long as they shall be necessary, will not, of course, exist in a watertight compartment. Our foreign policy will be determined by the people through their representatives in such a way as to serve two interests: those of the Greeks and those of peace. I personally believe that both these interests will be better served by our close association to the European community.

The present dictatorship, if it does not last too long, may in the end prove to have been a good thing—negatively. It's amazing how much the Greek people have "ripened" under it. They now know what they are missing, and they will also know what the mistakes were that permitted the imposition of totalitarian rule. We can hope that these mistakes won't be repeated. There is a good chance that the democracy of tomorrow in Greece will be a sound one, which will really pave the way for a Greek renaissance, indications of which had already timidly made their appearance before April 21, 1967.

It has been said that the Greek people are indifferent and apathetic, that they do not wish to fight for the restoration of their freedoms. Sometimes this is said in good faith, sometimes just as part of the dictatorship's propaganda. I have never agreed with this view. The Greeks are an intelligent people; they have suffered so much through the years that they are reluctant to undertake the real fight unless they feel that something worthwhile and serious has been prepared that can ultimately overthrow the dictatorship. To say that there was no resistance in Greece, even during the first years, is far from the truth. Certainly it is not true now after the wonderful showing of the university students and, to a lesser extent, of other categories of citizens. Resistance there has been, and it has brought about results. Otherwise the prisons wouldn't be full of resistance fighters, and martial law would not continue to be in force after six years of dictatorship. Having been present at its meetings, I think I can say that the Council of Europe would not have forced the Colonels out of its ranks so quickly had the only issues been the absence of a Parliament and the lack of freedom of the press in Greece. The ouster came because of the undeniable bestial tortures inflicted on prisoners, on the resistance fighters. It is they who really won at the Council of Europe. The Greek resistance was and is in a position to achieve international results against the present dictatorship.

As I end this book the stirring news of the rising of the youth of Greece reaches us! I never doubted that this day would come. Once again the younger generation shows the way.

We will carry on the fight on all fronts, within the country and outside it. And we are convinced that our expectations will come true. Let the dictators of Greece know, let the world powers understand: the Greek people will settle for nothing less than liberty!

APPENDIX A
TORTURES

Much has been said and written on tortures in Greece under the present dictatorship. Good required reading on the subject, in the English language, is the report of the Council of Europe (Strasbourg, 1969), James Becket's *Barbarism in Greece* (Walker and Co., New York, 1970), Andreas Papandreou's *Democracy at Gunpoint* (Doubleday and Co., New York, 1970), John Katris's *Eyewitness in Greece—The Colonels Come to Power* (New Critics Press Inc., E. P. Dutton, 1971), and Lady Amalia Flemming's *A Piece of Truth,* issued recently in London.

I do not feel I can describe these tortures better than the actual victims can. Here I present parts of their testimony (I use Becket's English version, abridged in part). These are the stories of four men out of the hundreds that have been tortured. They are Gerasimos Notaras, political scientist, and

Stelios Nestor, lawyer, both of "Democratic Defence" (Centre-Left); Yiannis Leloudas, poet and archaeologist, of the "Patriotic Front" (Left); and Angelos Pnevmatikos, army officer, royalist (Right).

GERASIMOS NOTARAS

I do not admit the contents of my testimony made before the naval authorities, given that the greater part of this was made as the result of physical and mental violence exerted on me. In point of fact on February 2, 1968, namely at the time of the completion of the preliminary investigations by the Sub-Administration of the Athens Security, my case was referred to the Athens Court Martial, and I was transferred to Averoff Prison. Two policemen admitted me and conducted me to New Perama, where they handed me over to Lieutenant Kiosses, R.N., who was accompanied by two men of the Chaser Submarine Command (D.Y.K.), and by a man in civilian clothes whom I did not know. Subsequently I was taken aboard the battlecruiser "Elli," which was out of commission, where Lieutenant-Commander Kamarineas, R.N., and Major Theophyloyiannakos, of the Military Police, were waiting for me. I remained under investigation in this ship from the above date until March 8, 1968. Throughout this period I repeatedly suffered the "phalanga" torture [see Nestor's deposition, page 199]. Similarly I was repeatedly beaten throughout the duration of the investigation by the above-mentioned persons, as well as by men of the Naval Police, who, not satisfied with the previous beatings, came at night into the cell where I was held and beat me, demanding that I should admit and confess to the testimonies I had supposedly made.

Because I had mental endurance, and did not proceed to these confessions, they put me to the torture of electric shock, which was inflicted on me as I was stretched out and tied for hours on a metal spring mattress. In addition to all this they continually threatened that I should be drowned, as if by accident, if I did not confess. Throughout all this time a high-powered electric light was burning in my cell so that I could not sleep, and, from time to time, for the same purpose, the guards beat noisily on the sheet-iron of my cell.

Finally I declare that I was never allowed to wash or smoke or read, and only two glasses of water a day were allocated to me, with the object of weakening my physical and mental resistance, so that I should confess all that my questioners demanded.

Consequently the so-called "depositions" or "testimonies" do not constitute the product of my free will. They were extracted as the result of the above tortures, consisting of intolerable, illegal, and immoral physical and mental violence aimed at distorting my testimony on the subject of the activities of Politis, my co-accused, and at adding other acts which I had never committed, and words which I had never uttered.

STELIOS NESTOR

In the early morning of May 24, 1968, agents of KYP (the Greek equivalent of the C.I.A.), dressed in civilian clothes, arrested me after entering my house carrying revolvers. Certain of them took me to the Chief of KYP, while others took the keys of my office, where, without my presence, or that of anyone else, they made a search, taking from my files whatever they considered useful. After a few minutes' stay at Headquarters, I was taken by car to the National Security Police of Salonica, where I remained for about half an hour. From there KYP agents took me over and, when they had handcuffed me, they put me in a car and covered my head with a piece of cloth. The car set off towards the east of the city, took the road to the airfield, turned at the Agricultural School crossroads, and entered the camp near Sedes airfield. Although my face was covered, I was able to determine the place where they took me to because of characteristic details of the journey, such as certain turnings, and points with distinctive lighting, which I could make out through the cloth over my eyes.

At the gate of the camp the guards had a few words with my escort and allowed the car to pass, a certain sign that the camp was not unaccustomed to nocturnal visitors. When the car stopped I was taken, with my face still covered, to an enclosed room, where the cloth was removed. Before and during the whole journey my escort advised me to tell what I knew so that I should not be tortured.

In the room I found myself in the presence of four or five people. One of them, tall and heavily built, approached me and punched me hard in the stomach. At that moment a short young man came in, who, as I ascertained later, was Captain Kourkoulakos, who served in the KYP. He warned me that if I did not speak, I should be responsible for whatever followed. On my refusal to answer, they ordered me to take off my shoes and two of the men brought in a rifle. They put my legs, at the ankles, between the rifle and the strap. Then they lifted the rifle to such a height that I was hanging upside down with my bare soles uppermost. The tall man then took a thin whip and began to beat my soles, while Captain Kourkoulakos at every blow asked me various questions about people and things. After the first phase of the beating they raised me upright and ordered me to stamp heavily on the cement floor, which had been made wet before. After this stamping my feet swelled. Then the hanging upside down and the beatings were repeated. This proceeding was resumed several times. [This is the "phalanga" torture.]

Each time I lost consciousness a bucket of water was thrown over my face. When finally my feet had open wounds from the beating, they lifted me up, and, because I could not stand upright, they put me, half fainting, up against the wall while two men hit me on the face and pulled hair out of my moustache.

I have no accurate idea of the duration of my torture. I remember, however, that at some moments when they had me hanging and were beating me with a whip, I felt severe pain in my chest, and had intense difficulty in breathing. My torturers were then afraid that I would die and stopped. I was soaking wet, and they transferred me to a cell in the detention premises of the KYP, where I stayed for the remaining 47 days of my interrogation. The day after I was taken to this cell, because I could not get up and my clothes were soaked in blood, they wrapped me up in a blanket and took me over to the office of KYP Major Anastassios Papakonstantinou, where I was again questioned. Although he saw my condition, he expressed no surprise whatever. The following days they provided no medical help, although I complained to someone who visited me that I felt pain from the probable dislocation of toes of my left foot. On the contrary I was compelled to go almost crawling for my bodily needs to a filthy lavatory, at the risk of infecting my wounds. As a result of this beating, the joint of the second toe of my left foot was dislocated.

Besides the physical torture, I was also subjected to mental violence with the purpose of extracting confessions. Thus, a week after I was arrested, Papakonstantinou and Kourkoulakos threatened that if I did not speak they would arrest my wife. Subsequently they gave orders in my presence to an agent to arrest my wife and bring her to the torture chamber to undergo the "phalanga." My cell measured about three feet by ten feet and a half. After having been held in it for 47 days, at the end of the preliminary interrogation I was sent, together with five other detainees, to a basement cell of the Transport Branch of Salonica for three and a half months. This cell was without natural light, and because there was no sufficient space, we were compelled to spend twenty-one out of twenty-four hours lying or sitting on the floor. Throughout the whole of my imprisonment in the Transport Branch we were allowed to go out for an hour and a half in the morning, and as much in the afternoon, into a small sunless courtyard.

I will not refer here to the omissions and irregularities of the proceedings, which were an obvious violation of the principles of legality, and establish them as clearly invalid. I declare, however, that I am willing to confirm from the beginning, to explain and expound to any competent agent of the Council of Europe, all I report in the present statement.

YIANNIS LELOUDAS

This document is intended to serve as testimony on the current and systematic use, by the Security Police and other agencies in Greece, of various methods of inflicting physical pain over a sustained period of time, of psychological intimidaton, of privations beyond the simple privation of liberty, and of generally inhuman and degrading treatment, against opponents of the present Greek government. In it will be recounted in some detail my personal experiences at the hands of the Athens Security Police, and only such instances of the above as have been actually seen or heard by me.

Immediately following my arrest, and having refused to disclose information which would have led to the capture of at least one of the people involved in the resistance network I worked for, I was threatened with execution on the spot. I was blindfolded and carried to the "spot," where, having waited for an amount of time which I am unable to calculate in terms of clock time, instead of the shot I expected, I started receiving blows all over my body (except those parts where the blows might have caused a bone to break) by means of a wooden log, which I felt to swell to unnatural proportions as the blows went on. I later understood that it was not the log which kept swelling with each blow, but my own body. As I was still blindfolded, and wishing to awake some sort of shame in my torturers, I asked them how many men it took to beat me up. Their reply, which I consider significant, was, "Seven. You are a liar, and we have the right to be seven to beat you," an indication that they considered this quite a normal state of affairs. I knew then that I had moved into another universe and that I could have no hope of the least communication on common human premises. From then on we both had very definite jobs to do: they to torture, and I to be tortured; which is what happened for what I calculate to have been five continuous hours. Very soon the method of torture they resorted to was the "phalanga." I was subjected to this basic and most widely used method of torture naked, except for my underpants, gagged at times, when they thought that I was ready to scream my pain out, continuously menaced with further more elaborate methods of torture, such as impalement, if I did not "talk," insulted with the foulest epithets in the Greek language, hit and kicked all over my body, including my stomach, testicles, and face, even though they were particular about not leaving any marks on my face, and finally shot at at close range and close enough to make their menace of killing me plausible, without touching me. My instinct of self-preservation managed at the time to persuade me that the shots fired were blanks, although now I cannot really believe that Security Police officers go round with pistols charged with blanks. There were twelve or thirteen persons actively involved in this, alternating as the one in charge of the feet got tired, and relaxing by kicking and hitting wherever they found a spot where there was nobody hitting. Inspector Vassilios Lambrou, head of the so-called Information Department, Lieutenant Petros Babalis, assistant to the same, directed and actively participated in what everybody seemed to consider, and actually was, a normal and ordinary working session.

I have at this point to describe what the "phalanga" consists of. The prisoner is made to lie on his back, and tied or held to that position, while he is being beaten on the soles of his feet by means of an iron or wooden rod, for a period of time depending on his physical and moral resistance, the torturer or torturers' ability to stand fatigue caused by his job, the importance of the questions asked, and the number of prisoners waiting to be treated. It is administered on shod feet, as shoes prevent the feet from being swollen to insensitivity or bursting open after the five minutes or so. Another measure usually taken towards the same end is making the prisoner stand up from time to time to walk or jump around, so that the muscles will work. It can be seen that the "phalanga" presents numerous advantages, which have made it the favourite form of torture. It ensures maximum pain through a relatively un-limited time of full consciousness on the part of the prisoner. People very often faint, or pray to faint, but they are immedi-ately revived. It leaves no permanent marks such as scars or broken bones. One notable exception to this rule is Apostolos Dakos, who limped through Averoff prison, in December 1967, the sole of his right foot burst open like an over-ripe fruit, the red and raw flesh visible even through his socks, and two of his toe-bones broken and crookedly mended through lack of medical help. Prisoners having been subjected to the "phalanga" are able to walk normally, and are presentable again in an interval of time which can extend from ten days to much more, depending on the person's age and ability to recover. Elias Bentzelos still had to regularly bathe his feet in warm water three months after he had been tortured, as the soles were still of a bluish hue and still aching. I was able to walk in about fifteen days. The "phalanga" can be administered once or re-peatedly at a day's or more interval. The person being brought in after treatment is carried by two or more policemen, or, in worse cases, brought down in a blanket. He is usually in a state of consciousness comparable to somnambulism. A young boy, whose name I cannot disclose as I do not know his present whereabouts, two hours after he had been brought down, having completely lost his sense of time, said, "They really went over me yesterday." A man who saw me being brought down, through a crack in his cell window, later told me that I moved like an automaton, having to be turned every time I headed for a wall which apparently I was unable to see. Another reason for this is that I was in such a state that my head could not possibly conceive of another movement or direction than that which at each moment I was set upon. Whenever a prisoner who has been tortured is brought down, prisoners not in solitary confinement are ordered into their underground communal cell, so that they will not be able to see him. Such orders are shouted at all times of the night, and there rarely passes a night without them. On one night I personally counted eight such orders.

After I had been subjected to the "phalanga" treatment, I was thrown into a solitary confinement cell, where I was kept for fifteen days. The cells used for this purpose in the Athens Security Police Headquarters measure 1.80 metres in length and something like 0.80 in width. There is neither light nor aeration and the prisoner has to provide himself with a blanket in order to lie on the filthy bare cement floor. These cells are full of bugs, which provide many a prisoner with a unique way to pass time: burning them up one by one with his matches. Many people pass quite a number of days under what is called "severe isolation." This consists of no nourishment, no water, no cigarets, no access to the toilet, and no blanket. I lived under this régime for forty-eight hours. One does not usually mind the lack of food, but the lack of water is excruciating, especially after torture which leaves one without an ounce of moisture in the body. I was fortunate enough on the second morning to fall on a guard who was either half-human or had not yet received his day's orders and allowed me to go to the toilet, where I managed to drink from the water pipe leading into the turkish toilet, my hands and lips touching the excrements others like myself had left floating there. I had to make water on the very cement floor on which I could not stand, sit, or lie down except by balancing myself on the only two parts of my body which were not raw with pain: my hip bone and my elbow. Naturally I was unable to sleep for four days. As soon as my exhaustion overcame me I lost that only humanly bearable balance and woke up immediately screaming.

But the worst part of being held in the Athens Security Police Headquarters is not one's own pain or thirst or suffering. It is the sounds. It is the screams of people being tortured, the moans, sometimes the weeping of your neighbours, the orders for the people not in solitary confinement to go down, and, more than everything else, the agonizingly soft, slow, five-minute, four-metre, interminable voyage on all fours of a tortured man whose name you do not know and whose face you cannot see from his cell to the toilet, and then the whole bowel-tearing thing all over again on his way back.

Political prisoners in Greece start being human again only when they are safe in prison. When Andreas Lendakis came to Averoff prison he was still trembling, with that interior trembling which is the residue of torture, physical and moral. It took him several days to be human again. But prison does not always give safety. I saw Ioannis Stratis the day he was brought back to prison from the Dionyssos camp, where he had been taken from Averoff prison. His face and one eye were still swollen and red. He too did not look human. Very few people do after they have undergone the treatment reserved to political prisoners in Greece.

This very small part of the truth which I have recounted, wishing to confine myself only to those things, tangible proof of which I have personally witnessed, is at least indicative of what I set out to make clear: that the use of torture in Greece is not incidental but systematic and carried to a scale as large

as the smallness of the country can permit, according to a pre-
conceived plan of which no one of the people actually ruling
the country can disclaim responsibility.

ANGELOS PNEVMATIKOS

I was arrested in Athens on March 22, 1968, and taken to
the General Security. Two days later I was transferred to regi-
mental prison (EAT/ESA). It was dark, the mattress hardly
fitted in the narrow cell. The interrogators worked in shifts.
March 25–26, 1968: Theophyloyiannakos slapped me twice in
the presence of Papageorghiou and madame Katina. April 2,
1968: They took my first deposition.

April 3, 1968: I was led to the Military Police Centre. It was
an old stable, which had been transformed into a jail. There
was the smell of urine everywhere. In the cell there was a bed
frame and three planks, no mattress and no blanket. It was
very cold. A soldier brought food, leaving it on the ground in
a tin can, without a spoon. Everything was disgustingly filthy.
He put the bread on the ground in the filth, and to one side
there was a pail full of garbage and human excrement. No
sooner had he brought the food, which I couldn't bring myself
to eat, than the noise of a motorcycle's motor started up right
outside the ground floor window. For three hours I was tyran-
nized by this infernal noise. This was repeated several times.
Nobody came to see me until the evening when a soldier came
and left food in the same way as he had before. All night long
they banged on the metal doors and the bars, and at the same
time my only light blinked constantly on and off. I stayed this
way until Saturday evening, April 6. Then the Commander,
Major Papageorghiou, paid me a visit. He spoke in a threatening tone, "Now Mr. Big Deal, why don't you confess? If you
don't you'll see what will happen to you."

He made me get in a jeep with two soldiers of the military
police, and they took me to Dionyssos, where the 505th Bat-

tallion is located. The commander is Yiannis Manouskakis. They took me directly to the detention cells at the far end of the military camp, at the foot of Mount Pendeli, under the trees. It was a low building with six cells, each measuring one metre by two metres-thirty, and two metres high. The building was covered with sheet metal; the doors were made of wood, and there were no windows. There was no natural light, nor electric light, there was a bed, a mattress, but no blanket. I had hardly been shut in when officers visited me one by one, dressed in shirts or sweaters, or just undershirts. They all carried pistols at their belts. Some of them wore civilian clothes and military boots, I suppose so I wouldn't learn their rank and identity. They had a powerful electric light which they flashed in my eyes when they asked me various questions.

Finally one came and ordered me to take off my clothes and my shoes. I refused to take off my pants, and told them an officer did not strip this way, and if they wanted to take them off they would have to do it by force. He went away. Because I was freezing from the cold I demanded to see a doctor for my heart and chest. It was on his advice that they later gave back my clothes, and I was allowed to wear a cotton undershirt and my shirt.

A dozen of them gathered outside my door and started making a tremendous racket, beating with metal rods and sticks on the sheet metal. They continued this for a long time, taking only short breaks of three to five minutes, during which an officer came in and demanded that I confess, because if I didn't I would be tortured. They ordered me again to take off my clothes. I refused. They started beating me with a club but I managed to grab it. Then they brought wild dogs that were held on chains and they goaded them, pushing them into the cell to bite me, shouting all the time: "Bulgarian traitor! Wretch! Communist! Fairy! You are going to die tonight! Cross yourself!" Shortly thereafter Candidate Officer Sideropoulos grabbed me by the throat shouting, "Just like the communists killed my father, I'm going to kill you, cut your throat with a piece of jagged metal!" All these insults, threats, and noises were made by a group of officers who were just outside my cell. These scenes lasted until three in the morning, when I heard someone who said, "He's not giving in. Me, I'm leaving, but you keep it up." He added something in a low voice, but I couldn't make it out. I heard a jeep drive off. It was probably Papageorghiou and Basil Ioannides who were leaving. (This last one belongs to the G-2 of the General Staff of the 505th.)

This situation lasted until morning, when the Commander of the third company came to visit me. He told me his name, though not his rank, and he wasn't wearing any insignia. He demanded that I confess. Toward eleven o'clock in the morning I was called to the office of the deputy-commander of the 505th. Major Basil Ioannides was also there, as well as the commander of the third company. They offered me coffee. They were all in uniform, and they demanded that I confess. They said I should reflect on what awaited me if I didn't. Since I refused I was once again sent back to my cell where every half hour there was the noise of the sheet metal, the attacks of the dogs, and the visits of the candidate officers. This went on without any let-up until the afternoon of Monday, April 8, 1968. It was then that I was called to the office of the commander of the 505th, Yiannis Manouskakis.

Up to this point I hadn't eaten or drunk water since the 3rd of April. He offered me some french-fried potatoes in his office, and said that everything that had gone on had happened without his knowledge and that it would not be repeated. Actually nothing did happen Monday evening, but it all began again next day (April 9). Before they began to beat me again, Major Koutras visited me and asked me to confess, and promised me that if I did, he would free my brother Costas, and the other prisoners. I refused.

Before I underwent "phalanga" Major Ioannides used the method of burial on me. "Angelos," he said, "you better confess, because you will regret it if you don't." Behind the prison is a trench in which they put individuals and cover them up with sand, leaving only the head unburied. The time of burial depends on the resistance of the victim. I cannot say how long I was buried there, because the anguish, the nervous strain, and the constant questions shouted by people working in rotation gave false impressions of time. Those that collaborated with Ioannides in this were the Officer Candidates Visanyaris and Sideropoulos. The battalion doctor supervised the operation from the medical standpoint.

Tuesday evening an officer candidate arrived who began to beat me with karate punches on the back of the neck and in the stomach. I hit back until a second one came and grabbed me by the thumb of my left hand, twisting it, while the two continued to beat me without pity until the next morning.

Then I was taken to the office of Ioannides. He was there along with the deputy-commander and the commander of the third company. Again I refused to talk and they led me back to my cell where I was beaten until the evening. At 20 hours they took me again to the office of the head of the 505th where Ioannides, the commander of the third company, and a captain, were waiting for me. They began to beat me with their fists and finally threw me into the office of the deputy-commander, in which there was a camp bed without a mattress. Some of the officers watched me while the others held me down. The whole operation was directed by Ioannides. They hit me on the soles of my feet. Then they took me to the office where I again refused to talk. I was taken back for more, and had three or four phalanga sessions until I passed out on the floor. They picked me up, putting me in an armchair, while they called a doctor. He ordered me moved to the infirmary, where I was taken care of until Thursday noon. It must be pointed out that I had not eaten since the 5th of April.

On May 15, 1968 they transferred me from the 505th to the EAT/ESA. On May 20 I was moved to the Military Police Centre, in the same cell as before. They brought me a table and a chair, and, three days later, a mattress. During all this time I had seen no one of my family and I did not have permission to take a shower or even wash until the 4th of May. Major Theophyloyiannakos threatened me that if I didn't speak, he would bring my brother's sons and tell them that their father was staying in prison, because that was what I wanted. At the ESA Lt. Col. Ioannides visited me, and repeated the same things.

On May 31, 1968 I was transferred to Salonica, at first to the 616th Infantry Battalion, and after, on June 1, 1968 to the Second Police Commissariat at Kalamaria, where I was put in solitary confinement.

APPENDIX B
PROCLAMATION OF
DEMOCRATIC DEFENCE

Let no one think that the Greek people could ever accept without protest such a fate as is now theirs, a fate that was decided by a clique of military plotters and their foreign supporters.

The Greek people have reconstituted their forces and reorganized their immense reserves. Already the struggle is launched, and to it they will bring whatever means are theirs to offer, whatever strength they have, whatever lives are needed.

And this struggle—our friends abroad should not fool themselves—will be a struggle in which all Europe is the stage. Ask of yourselves what suffering Europe might have been spared if fascism in Germany had been adequately opposed when first it reached power.

Receive this message of the Greek resistance, which comes from the heart of 80% of the Greek population which opposes the dictatorship now thrust upon it. We are ready now to die for the sake of our own integrity and so that we may again call ourselves, and be known as, a free people.

It is the duty of every democrat to publicise our proclamation and participate in the struggle which is now beginning—the struggle of the Greek people to regain their democratic rights and to rid their land of tyranny.

By whom is Greece now governed if not by men who are traitors to their oath and to their nation? And by what right is it governed except the right of force?

Democracy has disappeared from our country and the will of a few treasonable colonels has become supreme law. Behind those who have usurped power stand all the dark forces of fascism. After countless adventures caused by these same forces, we were moving towards elections, in the hope of a proper expression of the people's will: at that moment, and under the facile pretense of fighting the communist danger, the army seized power and established a tyrannical dictatorship. Their own actions stamp our present rulers as liars and dishonourable men. We have no hope that they will ever willingly give power back into the hands of the people.

We do not deny the defects of our past form of government, and, particularly, we accept that it functioned poorly. Most of its defects, however, stemmed from the absence at the core of the nation of an effective and integrated democracy.

LET US REMEMBER:

A. that Parliament never managed to exercise effective control of the army, although our constitution held that there should not exist any self-contained authority outside the control of the elected government;

B. the unacceptable involvement of the King in activities not anticipated by the constitution, so that he himself assumed the leadership of the right wing. In the final analysis, he is responsible for the abolition of constitutional order;

C. that the leadership of our army was taken by a clique

of narrow-minded, uneducated reactionaries, who sought to advance their personal aims, while proclaiming that they acted only for the régime. This clique prepared the way and founded a dictatorship in the name of the King, and with the King's approval;

D. the lack of a genuine conservative party in Greece. If those parties which represented Greek conservatives had made clear, and if they had proclaimed, their deep belief in parliamentary democracy, and their refusal to tolerate any violation of the constitution, then the situation today would not be as it is. Let us not forget that despite the good intentions of any members of the right wing, it was they who initiated the "Pericles Plan" and the "fraud and violence" of 1961, and that the interference has owed much to their connivance. Furthermore they sanctioned the reorganization of the army command on the basis of political standing, so creating a situation in which a few obscure colonels, apparently with C.I.A. support, could overthrow the national régime;

E. the lack of a democratic internal organization within the Centre party. This party undertook the responsibility for the great ideological struggle that was necessary for the restoration of democracy in Greece; and it won the first phase because of the enthusiasm of its leaders. But it failed to organize itself on proper party lines, nor did it take advantage of the numerous chances where it might have confronted the emerging dictatorship;

F. the position of the press, which continually modified its political stance to suit the petty interests of its editors, and which propagated their changeable affections to the exclusion of that free and objective examination of the nation's affairs, which is a necessary function of the press in a growing democratic society;

G. the quality of our Parliament. With a few exceptions the deputies were third-rate men, unprincipled and unequal to the responsibilities of national leadership. Parliament did not serve as the first defence of democracy, did not react adequately to intrigue against the régime, and was powerless to resist the corrosion of its own power. The height of this collapse was reached with the transactions of the summer of 1965. Governmental authority had become corrupted by internal and foreign agents determined to prevent the growth of a liberal parliamentary democracy.

Certainly wherever one looked—in the social services, in the armed forces, in the labor unions, in the civil service, in every sort of national organisation—there were glaring examples of the malfunctioning of democracy in Greece. But the problem to be solved was not that of how best to destroy a sick democracy, but of how best to give it strength. *It was the weakness of our democratic system, and not its excesses, that led us to dictatorship. And it is those who undermined democracy who are most to be blamed; not those who were ineffective in their attempts to make it stronger.*

AND WHAT IS OUR DUTY NOW?

It is certain—we hear and sense it everywhere—that an overwhelming majority of the Greek people resents and hates dictatorship and will fight for its abolition. The time for political organisation has come. This organisation is necessary both for the overthrow of the dictatorship, and for the formulating of a secure democratic basis for the future political life of Greece. In the strength of this organisation lies the sure guarantee that will guard us against political corruption and further dictatorship.

The struggle for the overthrow of the dictatorship will start gradually. Any form of opposition will serve it. Dictatorship must be, and will be, abolished. We seek the unity of all Greeks, of every element of opposition to the dictatorship. We represent a wide democratic army, the vast majority of the Greek people, and with this right we address this message to every Greek man and woman who believes in the basic democratic rights of the individual, in human integrity, in the restoration to Greece of its respect and of its freedom. We ask you to unite; to fight with us for the overthrow of this illegal, corrosive dictatorship, to labour with us for the establishment of realistic, integrated democracy worthy of our nation.

Greek men and women, the struggle has started again. This is a time for honour: the day will come when you will be counted for the deeds that you do now. Give us your hand. Gather around us now as resistance forms against this gang of sinister tyrants, who corrupt the true spirit of Greece and lead us towards destruction.

Greek patriots, fighters for democracy, unite with us in the struggle against fascism and dictatorship. Greece must be saved from disgrace!

July 1967

APPENDIX C
FIRST AGREEMENT
BETWEEN
DEMOCRATIC DEFENCE
AND PATRIOTIC FRONT

This is the text of a communiqué which was published by the underground press in Athens, in February 1968:

Since last November leaders of Democratic Defence and the Patriotic Front met and exchanged views on the better way of organising national resistance to the dictatorship. The two organisations, while preserving their full administrative, political, and ideological independence, and in view of the undisguised subjugation of the Greek people, under the virtual toleration of the international organisations* and the apathy of the democratic governments—notwithstanding the precious assistance of democratic humanity—have decided to continue their contacts and exchange of views and information more systematically, through the creation of a Coordinating Bureau

* This was written two years before the decision of the Council of Europe.

of anti-dictatorial struggle, composed of representatives of the two organisations, in order that Resistance may be coordinated and intensified.

The Patriotic Front and Democratic Defence ascertain that the indefinite prolongation of tyranny in our country daily aggravates the position of the working classes, entangles all the more the vital problems of the Greek people, and imposes the urgent mobilization of all the forces of the nation against the hated dictatorship.

The common goals of the two organisations are:

—The removal of the Junta from power, and its dissolution.

—The formation of a government of the common confidence of all the political forces and the resistance organisations.

—The release of all political prisoners.

—The full re-establishment of liberty and the human rights of citizens.

—The holding of irreproachable elections.

The two organisations reject the illiberal Constitution which is being prepared by the Junta, and believe that the amendment of the country's basic statute is not the work of the dictatorship, but that of the Greek people, after they have secured their sovereign rights.

Democratic Defence and the Patriotic Front call upon all the proud and free Greek citizens of all political tendencies to cooperate for the overthrow of the dictatorship, which shall be the task of all Greeks.

In order to achieve this aim the two organisations are ready to use all forms of struggle including the toughest. The time-old experience of the Greeks teaches them that "LIBERTY IS NOT AWARDED, IT IS WON."

INDEX

222 **INDEX**

Papaligouras, Panayotis, 23
Papamargaris, Theocharis, 119
Papanastassiou, Alexander, 34
Papandreou, Andreas, 21, 35, 40–44, 105, 113, 115–116, 189, 197
Papandreou, George, 17–20, 41, 43, 77, 84–86, 89, 91–93, 96–97, 102–110, 113, 115, 121–122
Papandreou, George A., 20
Papandreou, Margaret, 20–21
Papandreou, Sophia, 20
Papanoutsos, Evangelos, 97, 102
Papaterpos, Colonel Alexander, 119
Papaspirou, Demetrius, 119
Papaspirou, John, 8, 119
Pappas, Tom, 26
Papazissis, Victor, 119
Paraskevopoulos, John, 22, 93, 115–116
Paris, 69, 122, 151–52, 193
Patras, University of, 99
Pattakos, Brigadier General Stylianos, 21, 28
Paul I, 81–82, 88–89, 92, 103
Pedagogical Institute, 100
Peloponnesus, 64, 119, 151
P.E.A.N., 76
Pentagon, 42
Peponis, Sakis, 3
Pericles, 100
"Pericles," 214
Peridis, General, 119
Perna, Giancarlo, 153, 169
Pipinelis, Panayotis, 88–89
Piraeus, 8, 10, 30, 59, 60–61, 133, 141
Plaskovitis, Spiros, 35, 119
Plastiras, General Nicholas, 78, 80, 82
Plato, 44

Pnevmatikos, Lt. Colonel Angelos, 198, 207–211
Pnevmatikos, Costas, 209, 211
Politis, Andrew, 119, 199
Polikos, 10–11
Polychronopoulos, Sergeant John, 14, 49
Populist Party ("Laikon Komma"), 72
Potts, 26
"Prometheus," 22–23
Protopappas, Charalambos, 119
Pyrzas, Constantine, 119

Q

Quisling, Vidkun, 77

R

Rallis, Costas, 107
Rallis, George, 119
Rally, Greek, 82
Red Cross, 75
Rivero, Admiral Horatio, 26
Rome, 37, 169, 177, 180–181
Roosevelt, Franklin D., 71
Rostow, Walter, 26
Rozakis, Admiral, 5–6, 10
Rungieris, Brigadier General Christopher, 14–15, 53, 61–65, 129
Russia, 192; *see also* Soviet Union

S

Salazar, Antonio de Oliveira, 189
Salonica, 18, 21, 35–37, 45, 74, 85, 88, 94, 113–114, 119, 199, 201, 211
San Francisco, Conference of, 80
Scialoja, Mario, 153–54, 169, 171, 175, 179–181

S.D.E. (Socialist Democratic Union), 34
Security Battalions, 77, 79
Servan-Schreiber, Jean-Jacques, 5
Sideropoulos, Army Candidate Officer, 208–210
Simonidis, the Elder, 126
Sipitanos, George, 119
Skliros, George, 191
Smuts, General Jan Christian, 80
Smyrna, 83, 175–176, 179, 181
Soares, Mario, 189
Sofianopoulos, John, 80
Solomos, Dionyssios, 158
Sophoulis, Costas, 119
Sophoulis, Themistocles, 81
Soteriadis, 122
Sotis, Lorenzo (Titi), 153, 169
Soviet Union, 81, 93, 102; *see also* Russia
Spaak, Paul-Henri, 80
Spain, 98, 189, 192
Spandidakis, General Gregory, 22–23
Spanidis, Admiral, 119
Spiliopoulos, Gendarmerie Lieutenant, 10
Stalin, Joseph, 78–79, 192
Stephanopoulos, Stephanos, 22, 109, 115
Stern, 18
Stettinius, Edward, 80
Stratis, Ioannis, 206
Stylianou, Michalis, 122
Switzerland, 176, 180, 185, 187, 189

T

Talbot, U.S. Ambassador, Philip, 25

Tapinis, Commander (RHN) Spiros, 4, 10
Tatsis, Constantine, 89–90
T.E.A., 90, 130, 135
Terrenzio, Yolanda, 122
Theodorakis, Mikis, 35–36, 119, 151
Theologiti, Aphroditi, 67
Theophanidis, Gendarmerie Captain Eleftherios, 130
Theophyloyiannakos, Major, 198, 207, 211
Thucydides, 99
Totomis, Paul, 24, 26
Toumbas, Admiral John, 101, 108
Truman, Harry S., 80
Tsagarestos, Constantine, 119
Tsaldaris, Constantine, 80
Tsepapadakis, Brigadier General Harilaos, 3
Tsirimokos, Elias, 108
Tzevelekos, Panayotis, 7
Turkey, 72, 83–84, 147, 170–175, 178, 179

U

United Nations, 80, 189
United States, ix, 10–11, 23, 27, 59, 84, 102, 104, 120–121, 132–133, 143, 146, 189, 191–192; *see also* America
U.S. State Dept., 18, 26

V

Valsamitis, 127
Vassilatos, Gerassimos, 3, 7–11, 119
Vassiliou, John, 119
Velianitis, General, 120
Venizelos, Eleftherios, 69–70, 72–73, 82

Venizelos, Sophocles, 82, 92
Versailles, Treaty of, 69
Veryvakis, Eleftherios, 119
Vidalis, General Orestis, 119
Vima, 18, 113
Visanyaris, Candidate Officer, 210
Vlachos, Eleni, 7

W

Wallace, George, 104
Washington D.C., 26
Washington Post, 26

X

Xylouris, Menelaos, 5, 10

Y

Yalta, Treaty of, 79
Yiaros (Yioura), 28–29, 119

Z

Zannas, Paul, 35, 119
Zevgou, Mrs. Katy, 36
Zigdis, John, 36, 101
Zoitakis, General George, 23
Zurich, 180–181, 185